VANCOUVER'S VOYAGE

VANCOUVER'S VOYAGE

Charting the Northwest Coast, 1791-1795

R O B I N   F I S H E R

with photographs by Gary Fiegehen

Douglas & McIntyre
Vancouver/Toronto

University of Washington Press
Seattle

92 93 94 95 96   5 4 3 2 1

Douglas & McIntyre, 1615 Venables Street, Vancouver, British Columbia
V5L 2H1

CANADIAN CATALOGUING IN PUBLICATION DATA
Fisher, Robin, 1946–
    Vancouver's voyage
    Includes bibliographical references and index.
    ISBN 1-55054-023-8
    1. Northwest Coast of North America—Discovery and exploration—British.
2. Great Britain—Exploring expeditions.   3.Vancouver, George, 1757–1798—
Journeys—Northwest Coast of North America.   I. Title.
FC3821.F58 1992   917.11'04'2   C92-091168-4
F851.5.F58 1992

University of Washington Press, PO Box 50096, Seattle, Washington 98145-5096

Library of Congress number 92-53590

Editing by Saeko Usukawa
Design by Barbara Hodgson
Typeset by The Typeworks
Printed and bound in Canada by Hemlock Printers Ltd.

FOR KERRY HOWE,

IN RECOLLECTION OF PACIFIC SHORES

CONTENTS

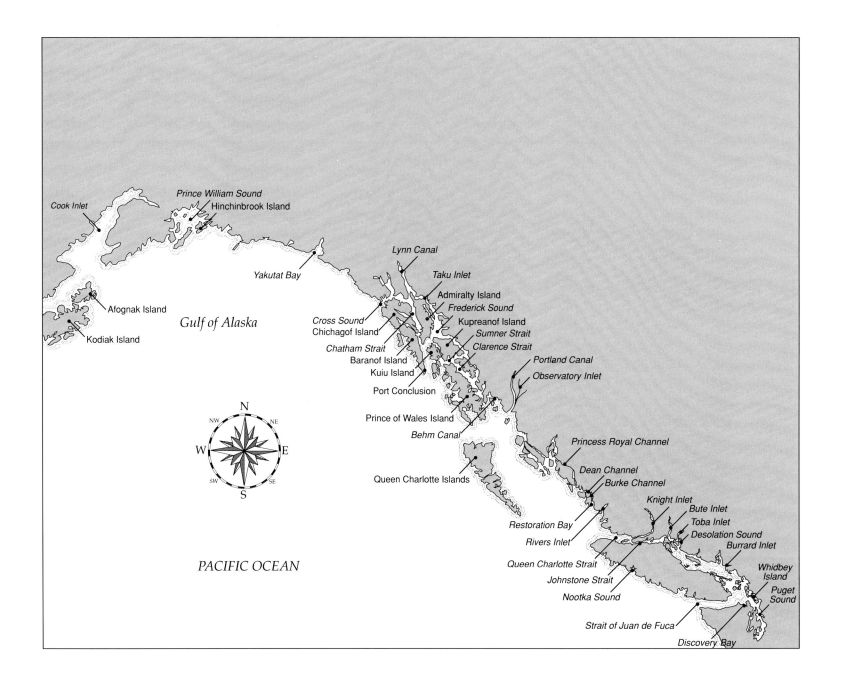

Cook Inlet

Prince William Sound
Hinchinbrook Island

Yakutat Bay

Afognak Island

Gulf of Alaska

Kodiak Island

Lynn Canal

Taku Inlet

Admiralty Island
Frederick Sound
Kupreanof Island
Sumner Strait

Cross Sound
Chichagof Island

Chatham Strait

Baranof Island
Kuiu Island

Clarence Strait

Portland Canal

Observatory Inlet

Port Conclusion

Prince of Wales Island

Behm Canal

Princess Royal Channel

Queen Charlotte Islands

Dean Channel
Burke Channel

Knight Inlet
Bute Inlet
Toba Inlet
Desolation Sound
Burrard Inlet

Restoration Bay

Rivers Inlet

Whidbey Island

PACIFIC OCEAN

Queen Charlotte Strait

Johnstone Strait

Puget Sound

Nootka Sound

Strait of Juan de Fuca

Discovery Bay

N
NW   NE
W   E
SW   SE
S

PREFACE

THIS BOOK APPEARS AT A TIME WHEN, for many, "exploration" and "discovery" have become dirty words. In 1992, two hundred years after Captain George Vancouver's arrival on the west coast of North America, we can no longer celebrate the achievements of European explorers with a clean conscience. Native people have forcefully reminded us that their rich and vibrant cultures were here for hundreds of generations before the newcomers appeared on their shores and that today they have little reason to commemorate the coming of Europeans. Clearly, for the original inhabitants of the northwest coast, ten thousand years is not a bicentenary. Among non-native North Americans, the controversy over the five-hundredth anniversary of the coming of Christopher Columbus in 1492 has created a legion of instant historians eager to assume that his mistreatment of native people in the Caribbean was typical of all parts of the continent ever since. As is often the case when the past is shaped to serve the needs of the present, history is distorted.

There is no doubt that history must be constantly reassessed, but at the same time it is not to be denied. Captain George Vancouver did arrive on the northwest coast on 17 April 1792 in command of a naval expedition sent by the British government to explore the coast and to resolve a disagreement with Spain. Of course, neither his coming, nor that of any other European, marked the beginning of discovery. Having lived there for thousands of years, native people were at one with the coast and knew its ways. Yet Vancouver still learned much that was new to him. He delineated the coast as a continuous line from Baja California in the south to Cook Inlet in the north. And, though he was not a particularly sensitive observer of the cultures of the coast, he slowly recognized some of the similarities and differences between the various peoples. Thus, for better or worse, he contributed to the revelation of the coast and its people to the wider world.

Vancouver also participated in a process of mutual discovery as natives and newcomers began to learn about and adjust to each other. The history of early contact on the west coast of North America was different from the experience in the Caribbean at the end of the fifteenth century. The early fur trade on the coast was a joint enterprise that may have been a mixed blessing for the native people, but did not result in the wholesale destruction of their cultures. Later in their history, the first nations people would be deprived of their land and resources, and there can be no doubt of the oppression that they have suffered. And yet, as natives and non-natives on the west coast now struggle to come to terms with their mutual past, it is important to remember that there were moments of accommodation and co-operation between them. If we are to look to the past for lessons for today, we must be sure that the complexity and colour of history are not lost to dogmatic assertions made in black and white.

Vancouver's Voyage presents one view of George Vancouver and the history of the northwest coast of North America in the late eighteenth century. I have relied heavily, though not exclusively, on Vancouver's own account of his voyage. While Vancouver's personality is not easy to penetrate, it is clear that he was not a paragon of virtue, nor was he a monster. He was only human and he had mixed motives, which is why what he did and thought while he was on the coast two hundred years ago still speak to us today. This book does not present the only view, nor is it necessarily a correct view, but naturally I believe it is a legitimate view. There will be others. I have not presumed to speak for native people, though I have not excluded them from this account. There are many voices from the past, and none should be silenced.

* * *

This book is published in conjunction with the Vancouver Conference on Exploration and Discovery held at Simon Fraser University in April 1992. When planning began for the conference, we were determined to find ways to bring the history of the coast to a wider audience than the academics who would attend the conference sessions. If it had been left to me alone, however, this book would never have become more than an interesting idea. Fortunately, others turned it into reality. First and foremost, the generosity of William Anderson made the research and photography possible, and, as a result of his donation, a copy of this book will be sent to every public and secondary school library in British Columbia.

I next took the idea to Scott McIntyre, of Douglas & McIntyre, whose boundless enthusiasm gave it life. Scott introduced me to the photographer, Gary Fiegehen, and I had the pleasure of working with both of them as the book took shape. I am still a little envious of Gary, who spent much of the summer travelling the length of the coast while I sat in my study and wrote; but when he returned, I was able to share his experience through his superb photographs. Gary Fiegehen's special vision of Vancouver's coastline today is presented in the colour plates that follow. Many people assisted Gary's travels, including Yvonne Marshall and Ray Williams at Nootka Sound, Ian Pepper and John Penner of the British Columbia Ministry of Parks, Jennifer Carpentar, Greg and Shay Foster, John Sisk of Alaska Discovery, Art and Linda Hayes of Glacier Bay Airways, Dale Pihlman and Cindy Ross Barber of Outdoor Alaska, Rick Blacklaws, Bob Herger, and Christiane Bohne.

The eighteenth-century illustrations came from a variety of sources. Many of the original drawings are from the Hydrographic Office, Ministry of Defence, Taunton, England, and the Bancroft Library, University of California, Berkeley. I am particularly grateful to Andrew David, not only for his hospitality in Taunton but also for facilitating my access to the Hydrographic Office. Other original illustrations were provided by the Public Record Office, Kew, the National Maritime Museum, Greenwich, the National Portrait Gallery, London, the Dixon Library, State Library of New South Wales, Archivo General y Biblioteca, Ministerio de Asuntos Exteriores, Madrid, James P. Ronda and Paul Richards. P. R. Sandwell, and Gene Bridwell of Special Collections at the Simon Fraser University Library, both generously allowed me to borrow their first editions of Vancouver's *Voyage of Discovery* so that reproductions could be made of the engravings and charts.

I am indebted to W. Kaye Lamb, the pre-eminent Vancouver scholar whose masterful Hakluyt Society edition of the *Voyage*, like Vancouver's chart of the coast, provides the sailing directions for those who follow in his wake. I am grateful to Kaye for taking the time to read my manuscript and for the benefit of his thoughtful commentary. Andrew David, Hugh Johnston, and Glyn Williams also read and commented on the text. Edward Ingram was, as ever, forthright and helpful. I trust that he now regrets the lost opportunity to do more. The final version and the appearance of the book owe much to the expertise of Saeko Usukawa and Barbara Hodgson. Mary-Ellen Kelm was at once my most formidable and caring critic. And, finally, *Vancouver's Voyage* is dedicated to a good friend and true colleague.

VANCOUVER'S VOYAGE

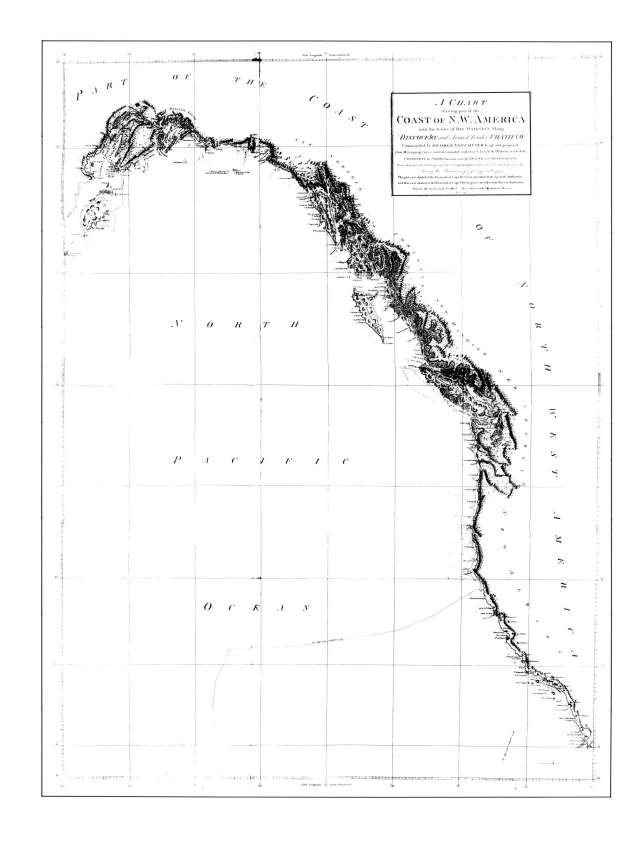

A CHART
shewing part of the
COAST of N.W. AMERICA
with the tracks of HIS MAJESTY'S Sloop
DISCOVERY and Armed Tender CHATHAM
Commanded by GEORGE VANCOUVER Esq.r and prepared
from the foregoing Survey under his immediate inspection by Lieut.t Jos.h Baker, in which the
CONTINENTAL SHORE has been carefully TRACED and DETERMINED,
From Lat 39.20 N. and Long 236.26 to Cape Douglas in Lat 58.20 N. and Long 207.20 E.
during the Summers of 1792, 1793 and 1794.
The parts not shaded to the Eastward of Cape Decision are taken from Spanish Authorities,
and those not shaded to the Westward of Cape S.t Hermogenes are taken from Russian Authorities.

I

Line of Time

IN THE BEGINNING, there was sea and land. And because both were vast and powerful, there was bound to be conflict at the place where they met. From the dawning of time, they contended against each other: water and weather assaulted the land, and the land retreated or resisted. Then, for thousands of years, the land was shaped and scoured by a crushing blanket of ice. When the ice finally receded to reveal its handiwork, there were no straight edges. The coast was an intricate thread of inlets and islands, of beaches and bays. Even though it was complicated and convoluted, the coast was a line that would be drawn inexorably through history. The meeting place of tide and time, it both marked a boundary and invited crossings.

The west coast of North America could provide moments of complete serenity, but it was not a benign place. When the gales ripped in from the Pacific, the coast could rage and storm like no place on earth. Even sailors who came only in summer knew its many moods. One such mariner, approaching the coast on 16 April 1792, instantly felt its anger, as if the land resisted his coming. In the middle of the night, as the elements roared around his vessel, he "stood on a wind until day-light," waiting for more favourable weather. Compared to the safety of the open ocean, a coast could be a dangerous place for a sailor. On-shore winds, reefs and rocks could all spell disaster, so he drew in carefully. When the storm subsided, he unfurled his sails and moved closer in towards the land. Driftwood and seaweed floating in the water and shore birds flying overhead heralded his approach to the coast. Still he was prevented from seeing the land by the weather which became "thick and rainy." Then, late in the afternoon, he got close enough that his soundings reached bottom: "The land was now discovered bearing by compass from E.N.E. to E. by S. at the distance of about two leagues, on which the surf broke with great violence."[1]

Captain George Vancouver had reached the coast of what he called New Albion, near Point Cabrillo, about one hundred miles north of what is now San Francisco Bay. In his own way, he knew exactly where he was. By dead reckoning, the longitude was 231° 30′ and the observed latitude was 39° 20′ north. Nor was Vancouver surprised that the coast could be turbulent. He had been there fourteen years earlier, a member of another expedition that had to find shelter from Pacific storms. For as a young man, Vancouver had learned his navigation from Captain James Cook, the greatest explorer of his time. Yet, in spite of the visits of Cook and others, much of the coast was still unknown to Europeans, so Vancouver was there to gather new knowledge. Over the next four years he would examine its entire length—from Baja California in the south to Cook Inlet in the north—in greater detail than anyone had ever done before. He came to the coast in a sailing vessel named *Discovery*, and his published account of the expedition would be entitled *A Voyage of Discovery*. In one sense the word "discovery" was a misnomer, since the coast was not unknown to those who were already there. In another sense it was appropriate, because his would be a voyage of mutual discovery, as the coast became a line for the meeting of cultures.

The people of the coast had been living there for at least ten thousand years before Vancouver arrived. Scholars say they came down from the north in search of easier living in a gentler clime. Or perhaps it was simply that the Raven, having rearranged the universe, was strutting down the beach one day and discovered the people trapped in a clamshell, struggling to be free. However they came to the coast, they decided to stay and learn its ways. They found that much of the shoreline was rich and abundant if they shared its secrets and responded to its rhythms. Living and moving according to the coast's seasonal round, the people gathered its resources in summer and explored its mysteries in winter. In villages that they built facing the sea, they established rank and order, ritual and art: in a word, civilization. And the cultures reflected the coast, for they were rich and vibrant.

As the people prospered and their numbers increased, the coastline became one of the most densely populated parts of the continent. Stretched out along the extended littoral, the indigenous peoples developed distinctive ways of life that were both unique to the coast and different from each other. To some degree this cultural diversity was imposed by the natural environment, for the coast both joined and divided communities. Though the sea formed the connecting link, groups were separated by the broken topography of the land. Parts of the coast were temperate and lush, while others were cold and harsh. In places it gave generously to the people, and living was easy; in others it was stingy, and life was a struggle.

The coast imposed conditions, but the cultures were the work of human ingenuity. Groups such as the Nuu-chah-nulth, Kwakwaka'wakw, Heiltsuk, Tsimshian, Haida and Tlingit were separated by distinct, mutually unintelligible languages. Rivalry over power and status was a driving force both within and between communities. While not always constant, the boundaries dividing groups were well defined, and the rights to use valued resource-gathering locations clearly understood. Disagreements could lead to warfare, even between peoples who spoke the same language, and it was usually waged to revenge insults or capture slaves. The societies were ordered and ranked in different ways, patterns of ritual were seldom exactly alike, and styles of art varied considerably.

Though their lives were different in a number of ways, the native peoples all had the coastline in common. They harvested most of their food from the water: the sea, the beaches and the rivers. For many, salmon was the staff of life, though they also caught other fish such as halibut, herring and oolichan. Hunters captured seals, sea lions and sea otters, and some ventured out from sheltered coves to harpoon whales on the open ocean. Along most of the coast, people took to the water in huge dugout canoes, each made from the trunk of a single cedar. In the coldest places, where the trees were small or did not grow at all, the inhabitants became very adept at manoeuvring flimsy little craft made from the skins of seals. The fruits of gathering supplemented the food acquired by hunting and fishing. The people picked clams, mussels and other shellfish from the beaches, and harvested seaweed along the shoreline. In spring, they collected herring roe by laying cedar boughs in the water.

The land was less important than the water as a source of food, though some animals were hunted or trapped. A wide range of plants, particularly berries and roots, yielded nourishment, while others were valued for their healing qualities. Growing along much of the coast, the cedar tree provided shelter, clothing and utensils: its wood split clean and true into planks for houses, and its bark and roots were skilfully woven into baskets and hats. But for all that came from the land, it was the sea that gave life. On many parts of the coast, the land seemed dark and foreboding, the dwelling place of malignant spirits who sometimes came out of the forest to threaten the people. On the coast, natural and supernatural were in harmony, for in mythic times the people and animals had been one. For hundreds of generations the people of the coast had adapted and endured, and they saw the turning of time in the ebb and flow of the tide and the circle of seasons.

LYN REGIS

Saylmaker del.   I King exc.   Kip Sculp.

In the eighteenth century, King's Lynn was one of the busiest ports on England's east coast. COURTESY PAUL RICHARDS

Then, suddenly, in what Europeans knew as the late eighteenth century, newcomers came to the coast. They came from distant lands, searching for new opportunities in what they were pleased to call the new world. These voyagers came from afar, in from the sea, while the people of the coast stood on the shore to receive them. It was a critical time in the history of the native people. The presence of newcomers on the coast would change their way of life forever as they were drawn into the wider world of trade and empire. Yet their cultures did not suddenly collapse. Their shoreline was as old as Europe and their civilizations as firmly established. They responded decisively to the European presence and shaped it to their needs. The people of the coast had already learned to evolve and adapt, so their cultures were dynamic at the moment of contact. At home in their world, the native people were confident and assured. The visitors were aliens on a foreign shore and, finding much that was unfamiliar, were often tense and uncomfortable.

Like the people of the coast, George Vancouver grew up close to the sea. The Norfolk town of King's Lynn, where he was born in 1757, was one of the busiest ports on the east coast of England in the eighteenth century. King's Lynn was a thriving market and trading town at the centre of a rich agricultural area. Its narrow streets and alleys were lined with warehouses and the waterfront was crowded with ships. The Tuesday and Saturday marketplaces were the locations for much of the town's business. Vancouver's father worked as collector of customs in the imposing customs house built on Purfleet Quay the previous century. The countryside around the town stretched perfectly flat all the way to the horizon and had been drained to facilitate a regular patchwork of intensive farming. The River Ouse drifted placidly through this ordered environment to became the Great Ouse at King's Lynn where it flowed into The Wash. Between the bustling market town and the flat fenlands that surrounded it, Vancouver grew up in a place that bespoke human control over the natural world. The explorer later transferred the name of his home town to Lynn Canal, but the place from whence he came was very different from the west coast of North America.

At fourteen, George Vancouver was appointed to serve with Cook. He was a midshipman, or an officer in training, on the second and third of Cook's great Pacific voyages. Such positions were acquired through influence in the right places, and Vancouver's particular contact may have been another King's Lynn family, the Burneys. The father, Doctor Charles Burney, was a prominent musician who knew the Earl of Sandwich, the First Lord of the Admiralty. Burney's daughter, Fanny, was a well-known novelist, and the son, James, twice sailed with Cook as a lieutenant. Whatever the actual connection, Vancouver got the position as a midshipman because of family contacts, and he was fortunate to do so. Though Cook was an exacting taskmaster, the training was the best that could be had. First, Cook taught his midshipmen to be good sailors, sending the young gentlemen aloft with the able seamen to reef or unfurl the sails. Later, he instructed them in observing, surveying and drawing: the skills of navigation that enabled a captain to travel to a distant part of the globe and provide directions for others to follow to precisely the same place.

The first time Vancouver sailed with Cook, from 1772 to 1775, he went to the South Pacific. One of the other midshipmen who messed with Vancouver remembered him as "a Quiet inoffensive young Man."[2] During the voyage he came under the tutelage of the astronomer William Wales, who taught him such things as taking lunar distances in order to fix longitude. The expedition spent the summers

The Customs House on Purfleet Quay, King's Lynn.
ROBIN FISHER

tracking about icy Antarctic waters, searching for *Terra Australis Incognita*, the great continent that, according to speculative geographers, was supposed to exist in the southern hemisphere. In January 1774 the expedition probed to latitude 71° 10′ south, farther south than any person had been before. Vancouver later claimed that, by climbing out on the bowsprit at the right moment, he had been closer to the south pole than anyone else on board. When the weather became unbearably cold in the south, they headed north to spend the winters among the islands of tropical Polynesia. They also visited New Zealand, which Cook had circumnavigated and mapped almost flawlessly during his first voyage. After three years of sailing amidst islands and ice, the expedition returned to England.

A year after his second voyage, Cook left on his third. This time the destination was the North Pacific. Having disproved the existence of the southern continent, Cook was now instructed to search for that other favourite of the theoretical geographers: the northwest passage that was supposed to connect the Atlantic and the Pacific. Vancouver was a midshipman on the second ship, *Discovery*, commanded by Charles Clerke. After sailing up through the Pacific, the expedition spent a month in March and April 1778 refitting at Nootka Sound on the west coast of what is now Vancouver Island. During this first close encounter between Indians and Europeans on that part of the coast, each learned much about the other. Cook's dealings were mostly with the Nootka Sound group that had one of its summer villages at Yuquot, or Friendly Cove as it later came to be known by the Europeans. The people of Nootka traded nearly every day at the ships, and Cook and his men visited their villages. The Europeans found the native people were open and hospitable, though they were also tough-minded traders and jealous about protecting their property. For their part, the Nootkan people observed the departure of the vessels with the ceremony due to honoured guests. Leaving Nootka, Cook and his men sailed north to Prince William Sound, Cook Inlet and on through Bering Strait into the Arctic Ocean. At latitude 70° 44′ north, farther north than any European had ever been in that part of the Arctic, they were turned back by pack ice.

The expedition retreated south to rest and gather supplies in the Sandwich Islands, as Cook named Hawaii. The two ships anchored in Kealakekua Bay, a sheltered cove on the leeward side of the largest island in the chain. Vancouver was one of a shore party that went inland in an effort to climb the snowcapped Mauna Loa. Not wishing to outstay his welcome, Cook sailed away from the bay only to be forced to return when *Resolution*'s foremast was damaged in a squall. He was clearly less welcome the second time. In the growing tension between the seamen and the Hawaiians, Vancouver was twice involved in physical scuffles.

The situation came to a crisis when Cook went ashore on the early morning of 14 February 1779 to remonstrate with a Hawaiian leader over the theft of a cutter. Matters got out of hand, and Cook met his untimely death, hacked to pieces on the shoreline. Dispirited, the expedition continued without the great captain. First under Clerke and later under James King, they probed into the Arctic Ocean once more before turning and heading for home.

Back in England, Vancouver was promoted to lieutenant, and, during the ten years between returning on one *Discovery* and taking command of another, he served on a variety of ships in a number of places. Both during and after the American Revolutionary War, he was in the West Indies. By the end of his tour of duty, he was first lieutenant on *Europa*, the flagship of Sir Alan Gardner, the commander-in-chief of the station. Gardner soon became a member of the Board of Admiralty, and through his influence Vancouver was given command of *Discovery*. Others who had been in the West Indies with Vancouver would join him on his voyage to the Pacific, and the names of Puget, Whidbey, Baker and Mudge would all become closely associated with the Northwest Coast.

The Northwest Coast of America, as it was referred to in the journals of the newcomers, had changed in many ways during the fourteen years between Vancouver's first and second visit. Whereas the coast had been the exclusive domain of its native people, it was now opening up to the wider world with its competing forces and interests. European voyages of exploration like those of Cook and Vancouver, or La Pérouse and Malaspina, were expressions of the age of enlightenment: of Europe's quest for new knowledge and new economic opportunities. These men were sent out into unknown seas with instructions to return with a shipload of scientific information about distant places and peoples. Using the latest technology, they strove to determine the shape of the world: to fix upon maps the exact contours of sea and land. They examined and evaluated the resources of far-off shores with an eye to new commercial possibilities. And they observed the indigenous people, recording a vast amount of information, and misinformation, about their ways of life. But they were not seeking knowledge for its own sake. These explorers were the representatives of expanding European empires and were looking for lands to possess and people to exploit.

By the second half of the eighteenth century, the Pacific was the particular focus of this enthusiasm for expanded horizons and new knowledge. Cook's visit to Nootka Sound in 1778 was a major factor in stimulating a number of nations to develop both commercial activity and imperial interest on the Northwest Coast. And a clash between these various concerns was the catalyst that led to Vancouver's voyage.

When the published version of Cook's third voyage appeared in 1784, it drew attention to the possibility of a profitable trade in sea-otter pelts between the Northwest Coast and China. Lieutenant James King noted that some of the pelts, acquired by crew members from the people of the coast, had sold for as much as $120 in Canton. He then went on to offer specific and detailed advice on how to organize a fur-trading expedition and how to proceed once on the coast.[3] British commercial interests were not slow on the uptake, and the following year the first maritime fur-trading expedition arrived at Nootka Sound. The first few expeditions set the pattern of exchange. It was usually a triangular operation that involved bringing goods to trade on the coast, taking the sea-otter furs to China to exchange them for silk and spices, then taking those back to the home port. As the early expeditions made considerable profits, more and more traders arrived. Initially, the trade was dominated by the British, but by 1788 American traders were also coming to the coast. By the early 1790s more than twenty vessels were plying the coast every summer in search of sea-otter pelts.

Contrary to the expectations of some early traders who had not read Cook carefully enough, the people of the coast were not simple-minded savages who would part with dozens of furs for a few trinkets. Rather, they were experienced, astute traders who knew all about margins of profit and how to drive a hard bargain. Trade was not new to the native people, who had developed well-defined patterns of commerce amongst themselves long before the Europeans arrived. They quickly adjusted to this new tribe of traders, and the fur trade on the coast soon settled down into a regular pattern over which the Indians exercised a great deal of control. Whatever the preconceptions and intentions of European traders, it was Indian requirements that had to be met before furs changed hands. With more white traders on the coast and Indian demands escalating, the maritime fur trade became more competitive and profit margins less certain.

Along with these commercial developments, the coast was also becoming the focus of competing imperial rivalries. The Russians were the first on the scene in the far north. In 1741 Vitus Bering, after whom the strait that separates Asia from North America is named, was the first European to enter what was later called the Gulf of Alaska. The name Alaska came from an Aleut word meaning "the great land." Bering realized the commercial possibilities of the fur trade with China, and, through the rest of the eighteenth century, Russian fur traders moved steadily eastward along the Aleutian Islands, the Alaska Peninsula, and the islands and coast of the Gulf of Alaska. This Russian activity in the north prompted a Spanish response from the south. Beginning in 1774, before Cook's arrival at Nootka, a series of expeditions were sent north from the Spanish base at San Blas in Mexico to examine the geography of the coast and to assert Spanish claims to the area. By that time the Spanish empire was stretched to the limit, and expeditions were tentative and often poorly equipped, so they often achieved less than British explorers. There was also some French interest in the coast, expressed in the form of the ill-fated expedition of Jean-François de Galaup La Pérouse which anchored in Lituya Bay on the Alaskan coast in 1786.

But the Spanish were the most persistent, if not the most successful, coastal voyagers in the years between Cook and Vancouver. The earlier expedition of Juan Pérez in 1774 sailed as far north as Dixon Entrance before turning back. Pérez encountered and traded with native people off the coast of the northern Queen Charlotte Islands and again near Nootka Sound, but he did not land, and the contact was fleeting. The following year, Bruno de Hezeta and Juan Francisco de la Bodega y Quadra left San Blas in the vessels *Santiago* and *Sonora*. Bodega in *Sonora* anchored in Bucareli Bay on Prince of Wales Island where, as at three other places on the coast, he took formal "possession" in the name of Spain. Bodega probed as far north as Cross Sound at the northern end of the Alaska panhandle before he was caught in a violent storm and forced to retreat. A third expedition under Ignacio de Arteaga and Bodega y Quadra was sent north in 1779 and reached Afognak Island near Kodiak. Then followed a period of nearly ten years during which Spain, preoccupied with European matters, took little active interest in the coast.

With the development of the maritime fur trade in the late 1780s, the Spanish realized that they would have to act or lose any chance of maintaining their claims to the Northwest Coast. In 1788, Estéban José Martínez, who had been with Pérez in 1774, was sent to the Aleutian Islands to gather information about the Russian fur trade. Perceiving the Russians as a threat and worried about the continued build-up of the maritime fur trade, the Spanish decided to establish a permanent settlement at Nootka Sound. In spite of strong reservations about his ability as a leader, Martínez was sent north in early 1789 to set up a post. The Spanish did not realize, though they would soon find out, that someone else, with schemes of his own, had been there before them.

The previous year, the British fur trader John Meares had spent the summer at Nootka Sound. He claimed to have acquired a piece of land from Maquinna, the ranking native leader at Yuquot, which by now was the major trading village on the sound. The exact nature of this transaction is unclear, and it seems highly unlikely that Maquinna would have transferred ownership of part of one of his most important villages to Meares. Perhaps the Indian leader merely granted the British trader temporary access to a piece of land. In any case, Meares built some kind of habitation on the land and a small schooner named *North West America*, the first European vessel to be launched on the coast. When the season was over, he sailed to Macao to sell his furs and make arrangements for the following year. In China, Meares joined forces with another fur-trade entrepreneur, John Etches, and together they planned a fur-trading campaign. The stage was set for a clash at Nootka between British commerce and Spanish imperialism.

Martínez sailed into Nootka Sound at the beginning of May 1789 to begin work on his fort and to assert Spanish claims to the area. He found a vessel owned by the Etches-Meares consortium, the *Iphigenia*, in the sound along with two American trading vessels. After some deliberation, he arrested *Iphigenia* as a threat to Spanish sovereignty. Then, realizing that he did not have the resources to hold the vessel and its crew, he released them on condition that Captain William Douglas sail immediately for Macao. Douglas left Nootka but continued trading on the coast. A few days later *North West America* sailed unawares into Nootka Sound, and it too was seized. When Thomas Hudson arrived in *Princess Royal*, he was allowed to leave, though he too ignored the injunction against trading. Once the fourth Etches-Meares trading vessel, the *Argonaut* under James Colnett, arrived at Nootka, the sparks really began to fly. Both Colnett and Martínez were intemperate men, and one bullied while the other blustered. There was a violent quarrel, and Colnett and his vessel were arrested. A few days later Hudson naively sailed back into Nootka, and this time he was detained. Both *Princess Royal* and *Argonaut* were taken to San Blas. Meanwhile, the crews of the two American vessels watched all these high jinks as uninvolved, if not disinterested, bystanders. Martínez had decided that the Americans posed no territorial threat and chose to tolerate their presence. Then, before the end of July, Martínez received orders to abandon Nootka. All of these antics might have amounted to no more than a minor farce in a distant part of the world, if they had not been turned into an international incident in Europe.

Initially, the British government had only a vague idea of the events on the Northwest Coast. But then, in April 1790, John Meares returned to England in high dudgeon, ready to make his side of the story abundantly clear. He presented an inflated and inflammatory account of the events at Nootka Sound. In the absence of other information, the government was taken in by Meares's testimony, and public opinion was aroused by this apparent affront to British freedom of navigation in the Pacific. As the rhetorical volume and hysteria increased, Britain and Spain came to the verge of war over the Nootka Sound incident. But cooler heads prevailed, and the two nations stepped back from the brink; they found a face-saving device in the Nootka Sound Convention, signed on 28 October 1790.

FACING PAGE: *Portrait alleged to be that of George Vancouver, by an unknown artist.* NATIONAL PORTRAIT GALLERY, LONDON, NO. *503*

From Tahsheis we proceeded a few miles on our way home, when, arriving at a convenient little cove, we pitched our encampment for the night, and passed a very pleasant evening.

FACING PAGE: *The violence of the surf, which still continued to break upon the coast in consequence of recent tempestuous weather, not only prevented their landing on this point, but rendered their navigating this rocky region perilous in the highest degree.*

The convention provided for compensation for the arrest of the British vessels and for restitution of the land and buildings taken by Spain in the summer of 1789. It also affirmed the right of both parties to navigate, trade or settle on the Northwest Coast. The exact details of the territorial settlement at Nootka Sound were, however, left to be worked out by representatives of the two governments on the spot. Many of the details of the convention were vague, leaving plenty of scope for conflicting interpretation. This lack of precision was just one more reason why Vancouver's voyage would be one of discovery.

By the end of 1790, plans for a major British expedition to the North Pacific were well underway. The *Discovery* and a tender, the *Chatham*, had been appropriated for the voyage, and George Vancouver had been appointed to command the expedition. Captain Vancouver joined his ship on 16 December 1790 at Deptford Yard, where it was being fitted out for the voyage. Like Cook's ships, *Discovery* had been built as a merchant vessel and was about the same size. A practical, functional vessel, it was made for hard work. A Spanish commander who met Vancouver on the coast thought that "*Discovery* is a ship fit for the object of its voyage, . . . even though it is not a pretty ship."[4] At 330 tons she was bigger than Cook's *Discovery* but smaller than *Resolution*. At just under one hundred feet long, twenty-eight feet wide and about six feet of height between the decks, she would provide cramped quarters for upward of one hundred men, their gear and supplies. Still she was a good sailor and well suited for the task ahead.

Chatham, on the other hand, seems to have been selected largely because she was available, and was ill-fitted for her role in the expedition. About a third of the

FACING PAGE: *As we had no reason to imagine that this country had ever been indebted for any of its decorations to the hand of man, I could not possibly believe that any uncultivated country had ever been discovered exhibiting so rich a picture.*

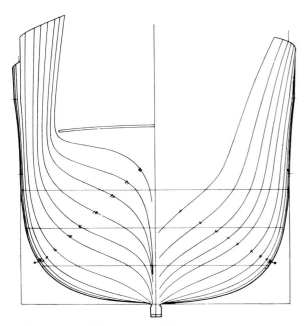

An elevation of Vancouver's vessel, Discovery.

size of *Discovery*, the brig-rigged tender was to be used for close, inshore sailing, but she proved to be very crank and slow. *Chatham* was so unstable sailing between the Thames and Falmouth that more than two and a half thousand pounds of shot were added to her ballast, and, when even this proved insufficient, twenty-three tons of shingle were added at the Canary Islands. Vancouver was constantly frustrated by *Chatham*'s slowness and, perhaps, by her annoying habit of nevertheless arriving at predetermined rendezvous ahead of *Discovery*.

Vancouver had more control over the appointment of the officers on *Discovery* than the selection of vessels, and he chose men he knew and trusted. His first, second and third lieutenants were Zachariah Mudge, Peter Puget and Joseph Baker. All had served with him in the Caribbean, as had the master of the ship, Joseph Whidbey. Vancouver seems to have had little say in the selection of *Chatham*'s officers: Lieutenant William Broughton was commander, his lieutenant was James Hanson and James Johnstone was master. There were a number of midshipmen on the voyage, young gentlemen in training just as Vancouver had once been. One of these, at least, he could have done without. The Honourable Thomas Pitt, later Lord Camelford, was a thorn in Vancouver's side throughout the voyage and after. Others, such as Thomas Manby, Henry Humphrys, Thomas Heddington, John Sykes and Spelman Swaine, were much more useful members of the crew. Humphrys, Sykes and Heddington would become the artists of the voyage and provide much of the visual record of the coast. Most of the able seamen on the expedition were there through the pull and influence of the press gang rather than men in high places. Many were reluctant voyagers.

Nor did Vancouver have much choice over the one civilian on the expedition: the naturalist and surgeon Archibald Menzies. He was there through the ubiquitous influence of Joseph Banks. Now the President of the Royal Society, Banks had been with Cook on the first voyage and had since appointed himself the custodian of the Cook legacy. He was a powerful advisor to the government and the Admiralty as the plans were being drawn up for Vancouver's voyage. Not only was Menzies Banks's man on the expedition but the twelve- by eight-foot glass frame built on Vancouver's quarterdeck to house botanical specimens would also be a constant reminder of Banks's influence. There would be tension between Menzies and Vancouver at several points during the voyage. Like Vancouver, Menzies had been on the coast before. He had spent the summers of 1787 and 1788 in the fur-trading vessel *Prince of Wales*, and he offered his advice on the choice of trade items to be taken to the coast on *Discovery*. But Menzies was aboard primarily as a scientist, the sole representative of that tradition of wide-ranging scientific enquiry established by Cook's expeditions. He was instructed to investigate the natural history of the lands he visited—the flora, fauna, geology and climate—paying particular attention to the potential for European settlement and commercial exploitation. He was also to be an ethnographer and report on the way of life of the native people of the coast. As the collector of scientific knowledge with Vancouver's expedition to the coast, Menzies was the servant of empire.

Vancouver's work on the Northwest Coast was to be diplomatic and geographic. His instructions were to sail via Hawaii to the Northwest Coast. There, his first assignment was to accept restitution from a Spanish representative at Nootka Sound for any land and buildings formerly owned by British subjects. More detailed instructions on the amount of land to be handed over were to follow in a storeship that would meet him in Hawaii. Once matters were settled at Nootka, Vancouver was to make a detailed survey of the entire coastline in an effort to find the northwest passage. He was to determine the general line of the coast and the direction and extent of inlets and rivers. He was to pay particular attention to the Strait of Juan de Fuca and Cook Inlet, which, in the minds of theoretical geographers, were likely entrances to a waterway that might connect up with the fur-trading areas around the Lake of the Woods or Hudson Bay in the interior of the continent. His survey of the coast was to be thorough, yet he was also instructed not to delay over inlets or rivers that did not appear to be navigable. He was given broad discretionary authority, and the Admiralty expected him to complete the survey in two years. In the event, it would take much longer. As a diplomat, then, Vancouver was to assert British claims to the area, while, as a navigator, he was to complete in detail what Cook had begun.

Discovery *as a convict hulk at Deptford in 1828.*
NATIONAL MARITIME MUSEUM, GREENWICH

"Friendly Cove, Nootka Sound...," sketch by H. Humphrys, engraved by J. Heath. VANCOUVER, A VOYAGE, VOL. I, P. 406

Complications & Convolutions

TRUSTING THAT THE DATE WAS NOT SIGNIFICANT, the expedition sailed from Falmouth on 1 April 1791. The objective was the Northwest Coast, but it would take them more than a year to get there. They sailed by way of the Cape of Good Hope where they put in for repairs and supplies, then on to the south coast of Australia where Vancouver surveyed three hundred miles of previously un-mapped coastline. Sailing up the Pacific, Vancouver's men were conscious that they were following in the wake of Cook. At Dusky Sound on the southwest coast of New Zealand, James Johnstone "was charmed with that degree of ac-curacy and exactness" with which Cook had surveyed the intricate maze of inlets and islands. Vancouver did fill in details of Cook's chart of the area, but felt that he could add nothing to what Cook had already written and so was left with "little else than the power of confirming his [Cook's] judicious remarks and opin-ions."[1] Vancouver discovered and nearly became entangled in the Snares Islands off the south coast of New Zealand but escaped to sail north to Tahiti.

There, the vessels anchored at Matavai Bay, just as Cook had done on all three voyages. This fabled, idyllic spot was eagerly anticipated by sailors ready for rest and recreation. The abundance of fresh island food made a welcome change from the dull shipboard fare, and, though Vancouver himself was unmoved, beautiful women seemed to offer the fulfilment of many a fantasy. At the same time, as vis-its by Europeans became more frequent, familiarity was producing a certain amount of contempt among the Tahitians. Vancouver decided to refit his ships and so stayed longer than expected: the sojourn lasted nearly four weeks. With Captain William Bligh's experience in mind, Vancouver kept a tight rein on his men, and, at first, all went well. But stealing by the Polynesians brought an over-reaction from Vancouver, and relations were tense in the last two weeks. Vancou-

"View of the North Promontory of Cape Mendocino...," monochrome watercolour by J. Sykes.
HYDROGRAPHIC OFFICE, TAUNTON, VIEW NO. 59

ver's health was deteriorating, even this early in the voyage, and he was prone to outbursts of violent anger. Though relations were finally patched up, both sides were probably relieved when the expedition left Tahiti towards the end of January 1792. Certainly Vancouver was glad to be finally heading for his objective in the North Pacific.

The next port of call was the Hawaiian Islands. Arriving off the coast of the Island of Hawaii, Vancouver passed by Kealakekua Bay with its gloomy memories and headed instead for Oahu. Rounding Diamond Head, he anchored in Waikiki Bay where the welcome for these visitors was muted and supplies were few. So Vancouver moved on to Waimea Bay on Kauai, the spot where Cook had made his first landfall in 1778. On successive visits to the islands, Vancouver took a great interest in Hawaiian affairs. He found both the place and its people more congenial than the Northwest Coast. Yet, even here, relations were not always smooth. Walking down the beach at Waimea, Vancouver interpreted some fires lit by the Hawaiians to burn off old vegetation as a sign of hostile intent and flew into one of his rages. In dealings with native people, he seemed to have a short fuse. Other arrangements were not going according to plan either. The storeship *Daedalus* was supposed to rendezvous with the expedition in Hawaii, bringing new supplies. When the gathering of food and water was completed and *Daedalus* had still not appeared, Vancouver decided to press on as he was already behind

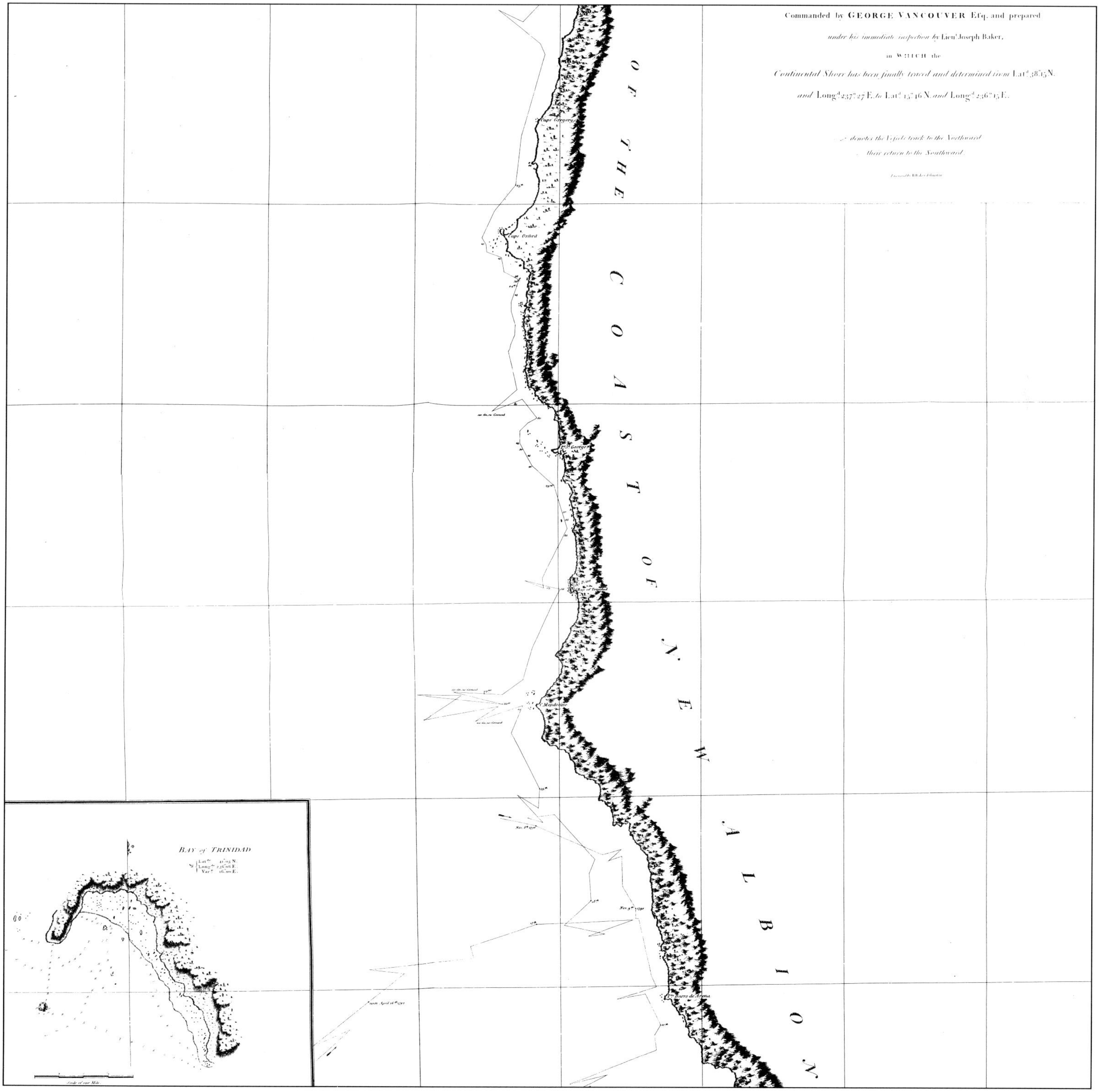

Commanded by GEORGE VANCOUVER Esq. and prepared

under his immediate inspection by Lieut Joseph Baker,

in WHICH the

Continental Shore has been finally traced and determined from Lat.d 38° 5. N.

and Long.d 237° 27 E. to Lat.d 15° 46 N. and Long.d 236° 15. E.

° denotes the Vessels track to the Northward

their return to the Southward.

OF THE COAST OF NEW ALBION

Cape Gregory

Cape Orford

Point St George

Mendocino

Barro de Pinas

BAY of TRINIDAD

Scale of one Mile

"View at the Entrance of the Straits of Juan de Fuca, Cape Claaset...," monochrome watercolour by J. Sykes. HYDROGRAPHIC OFFICE, TAUNTON, VIEW NO. 51

"View of Observatory Point, Port Quadra (Discovery Bay), Straits de Fuca," watercolour over pencil by J. Sykes. BANCROFT LIBRARY, BERKELEY, ROBERT B. HONEYMAN COLLECTION, NO. 600

schedule. He left word for the supply vessel to meet him at Nootka Sound and sailed for the coast of America to begin his work.

Hitting the Northwest Coast in mid-April, Vancouver decided to turn northward. He began by making a running survey of the coastline from Cape Mendocino to the Strait of Juan de Fuca, a technique he had learned from Cook.[2] The work was done from *Discovery* as she sailed up the coast. Running before the wind made the task relatively easy, but a head wind required constant tacking. Though the weather was sometimes foul, he tried to keep the land in sight during the day. Then the ships had to haul off and tack about in the offing during the night so that they could start at the same point the next morning. Vancouver and his officers kept a careful record of the track of *Discovery* and took compass bearings to prominent features of the shoreline. The bearings were then plotted from the appropriate position along the ship's track, the intersection of several bearings giving the true position of a particular feature. Due allowance had to be made for magnetic variation, which was obtained daily by observing the compass bearing of the sun and then calculating its true bearing. The rest of the coastline was filled in by visual observation. The midshipmen-artists made drawings of significant features of stretches of coast as a guide to other navigators, and soundings were taken frequently to measure the depth of the water.

Two features of Vancouver's work as a surveyor were revealed on this first stretch of coast: his blind spot on rivers and his devotion to Cook. He passed by the bay that forms the mouth of the Columbia River and has been criticized by those with the advantage of hindsight for not investigating such a major river more closely. Because the water changed colour, he suspected the existence of a river, but the bar of the Columbia was extremely hazardous with a line of cavernous breakers rolling over it. Following his instructions to concentrate on navigable waterways, Vancouver did not delay over the Columbia. Broughton did return in *Chatham* a few months later to explore the lower reaches of what he called the River Oregon. In the meantime Captain Robert Gray, an American, became the first non-native sailor to enter the Columbia River, which he named after his ship. For his part, Vancouver was still anxious to press northward to where the Strait of Juan de Fuca was supposed to be. Cook had passed by the latitude "where geographers have placed the pretended *Strait of Juan de Fuca*" and not only had seen "nothing like it" but also asserted that there was not the "least probability that iver any such thing exhisted."[3] Loyal to his mentor, Vancouver continued to doubt the existence of the strait until he rounded Cape Flattery and entered what he still referred to as "the supposed straits of De Fuca."[4]

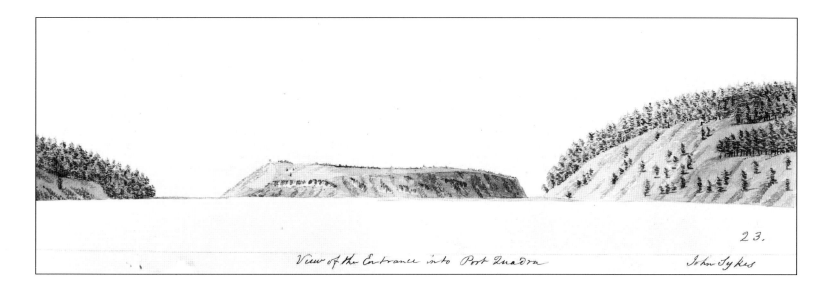

View of the Entrance into Port Quadra   *John Sykes*

23.

Having missed the major bays on the coast of what is now Washington, Vancouver was looking for an anchorage where he could refit his ships and rest his men. He sailed up the strait and found refuge in what he described as "one of the finest harbours in the world." He named it Port Discovery after his ship.[5] It is now called Discovery Bay. Once the ships were safely anchored, a shore station was established for astronomical observations, and the crews began repairing the vessels and gathering supplies. After a few days' work, the commander gave them all Sunday off to relax ashore. The weather was clear and serene, the sea was calm, and Vancouver felt at ease. He could not "believe that any uncultivated country had ever been discovered exhibiting so rich a picture." The scene was dominated by the snowy peak of Mount Baker, which Vancouver named after one of his lieutenants. Closer at hand, the landscape presented a variety of hills and valleys, forests and clearings. The land appeared to be bountiful, with verdant green meadows scattered among towering trees. There were numerous species of shrubs that would produce berries in their season, and many varieties of smaller flowering plants. Animal life seemed to be abundant, and the surface of the sea teemed with aquatic birds. Inevitably, "a picture so pleasing could not fail to call to our remembrance certain delightful and beloved situations in Old England."[6]

The peaceful respite was brief, and there were long days of hard work ahead. Port Discovery was well named, as it was the place where Vancouver began the process of learning about the coast. His plan was simple. He intended to survey

"View of the Entrance into Port Quadra (Discovery Bay)," watercolour over pencil by J. Sykes.
BANCROFT LIBRARY, BERKELEY, ROBERT B.
HONEYMAN COLLECTION, NO. 601

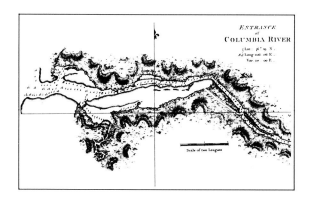

"Four remarkable, supported Poles, in Port Townshend,
Gulph of Georgia," sketch by J. Sykes, engraved by J.
Heath. VANCOUVER, A VOYAGE, VOL. I, P. 234.

every foot of the continental foreshore from the Strait of Juan de Fuca to Cook Inlet. It would be a prodigious task, and he wanted to get going. Since *Discovery* and *Chatham* were being repaired, he took out smaller boats to investigate the coastline in the immediate area. On this initial excursion the boat crews were provisioned for five days. Vancouver and Menzies were in *Discovery*'s pinnace, and Puget and Johnstone accompanied them in other boats. They began to chart the complex pattern of waterways around Puget Sound by first going into Port Townsend immediately to the east and then on to Hood Canal. It took five days to survey these two inlets.

"View in Port Townshend of Mount Baker,"
monochrome watercolour by J. Sykes.
HYDROGRAPHIC OFFICE, TAUNTON, VIEW NO. 53

Returning to *Discovery*, Vancouver began to recognize that mapping the convoluted coast would be time-consuming, exacting work. By now it was also clear that *Chatham* was quite unsuitable for close inshore work, and Vancouver became convinced that the coastline could be determined only from small boats. He came to this conclusion knowing that it would prolong the process and even though "such service in open boats would necessarily be extremely laborious, and expose those so employed to numberless dangers and unpleasant situations, that might occasionally produce great fatigue, and protract their return to the ships; yet that mode was undoubtedly the most accurate, the most ready, and indeed the only one in our power to pursue for ascertaining the continental boundary."[7]

Accordingly, the procedure followed on that first excursion soon became a regular routine. After the two vessels were anchored in a sheltered cove, an observatory was set up in tents on shore to obtain the latitude by observing the meridian altitude of the sun at noon. The longitude was obtained by numerous observations of lunar distances and by keeping a close watch on the *Discovery*'s chronometers. Magnetic variation was also obtained. From these calculations, the exact position by latitude and longitude was fixed. Meanwhile, crews in small boats were sent out to probe the inlets and circle the islands in the vicinity of the temporary base. They followed a procedure that was similar to the running survey Vancouver had conducted on the coast south of the Strait of Juan de Fuca. They rowed along the trend of the coastline, taking compass bearings of identifiable features of the land and careful measurements of the course and movement of the boat. The officers went ashore at intervals to take sextant angles of the direction of the coast and tangents to the offshore islands. All of this work was carefully recorded, and when the boats returned to *Discovery*, the information was transferred to a plotting sheet. Later, when the work in a particular area was completed, the information was added to a fair copy of the chart. Then the vessels weighed anchor and moved on to another location to begin the process again.

And so the survey began. When they were ready to leave Discovery Bay,

"View in Port Townshend, Streights de Fuca,"
monochrome watercolour by J. Sykes.
HYDROGRAPHIC OFFICE, TAUNTON, VIEW NO. 54

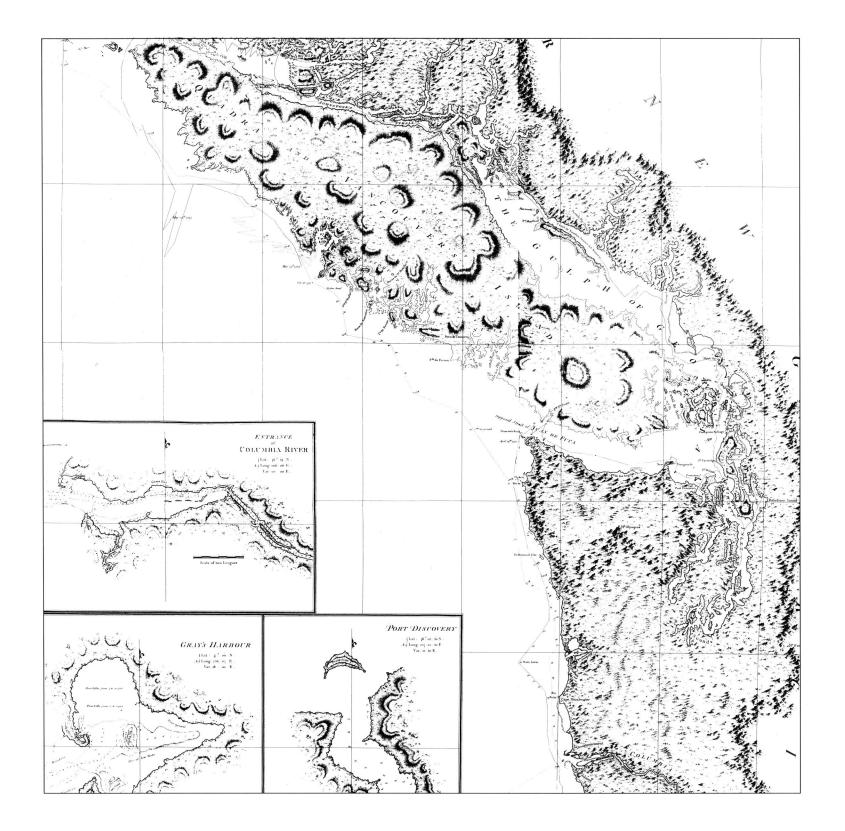

ENTRANCE
of
COLUMBIA RIVER

Scale of two Leagues

GRAY'S HARBOUR

PORT DISCOVERY

Chatham went ahead to reconnoitre the San Juan Islands while *Discovery* sailed into Puget Sound as far south as the site of Seattle. Further boat trips were required to map the rest of the sound. Though Puget was the senior officer on many of the excursions, Vancouver relied very much on Whidbey and Johnstone to carry out the actual survey work. All three left their names on prominent features of the coast during the first survey season: Puget a sound, Whidbey an island and Johnstone a strait. By the end of the first month's work, they had covered Puget Sound but had not advanced any farther north. In spite of the long days, the boat work could be pleasant when the weather was good, but when it rained, the seamen would be soaked to the skin for long periods and the task was tedious and uncomfortable. When *Discovery* and *Chatham* met up again at the south end of Whidbey Island, Vancouver, with the presumption common to all European voyagers of the age, named the stretch of water Possession Sound for the fact that he took formal "possession" of the area for Great Britain.

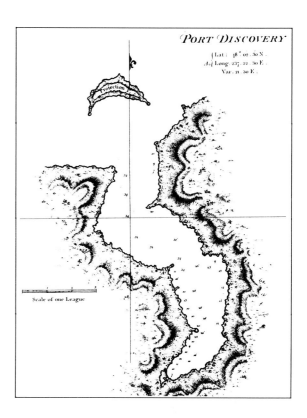

The people already living there naturally assumed that they were in possession of the coast. The expedition's first encounter with the native people of the Northwest Coast had occurred soon after they made landfall. Near what is now Cape Blanco, a group of Tututnis Indians who lived along the lower reaches of the Rogue River paddled out to the passing ships. These people were open and friendly. They were also forthright and honest in trade and had no interest in accepting trifling articles as presents. And soon after the voyagers had entered the Strait of Juan de Fuca, a group of Makah came off to visit the ships, and there were frequent encounters with native people by boat parties in Puget Sound. It seemed to Vancouver that these people approached his ships with less reserve and formality than the native people of Nootka Sound had done when he was there with Cook. Their changed demeanour, he concluded, was a result of greater familiarity with European visitors.[8]

While the Indians of the coast were becoming more familiar with foreigners, the reverse was not always the case. Vancouver himself was not a very sympathetic or perceptive observer of native cultures on the coast. He did not go as far as one of his midshipmen, Thomas Manby, whose first reaction was that the Northwest Coast Indians were "the nastyest race of people under the sun."[9] But Vancouver clearly intended to keep some distance between himself and the native people. Early on in Puget Sound, when groups of Indians had approached boat crews on the shore, Vancouver had a line drawn with a stick in the sand. He made it plain that he intended to keep the people of the coast on one side and his men on the other.

Vancouver's own boundary lines were both physical and mental. The physical

"*Mount Rainier from the South part of Admiralty Inlet
(Puget Sound),*" *sketch by J. Sykes, engraved by
J. Landseer.* VANCOUVER, *A VOYAGE,* VOL. I, P. 268

"View of a Boat Encampment, Pugets Sound, Straits de Fuca," watercolour over pencil by J. Sykes.
BANCROFT LIBRARY, BERKELEY, ROBERT B.
HONEYMAN COLLECTION, NO. 593

distance was kept out of fear. His first encounters with native people were friendly enough, like those of most early visitors to the coast, but he expected hostility and often exaggerated perceived threats. The mental distance came from lack of curiosity. Though he had ample opportunity to observe the people of the coast, he took little interest in ethnography, unlike some other European observers of the time. Initially, he drew on his earlier experience and compared all native groups to the Nootka Sound people. In spite of this point of comparison, he was slow to appreciate that a great variety of languages, and therefore cultures, existed on the coast. He was particularly struck by cultural features that were unusual and different from his preconceived expectations, once again emphasizing the lines of distinction between native people and Europeans. Not that he was completely rigid. For example, he was somewhat surprised to find that, contrary to the general belief among Europeans that all Northwest Coast Indians ate human flesh, some Puget Sound Indians had an aversion to cannibalism. In this case he did not question the general view, but rather put this particular instance down to differences between native groups. And Vancouver certainly did not place much credence on Indian testimony, even on simple points of geography. His opinion that "the little respect which most Indians bear to truth, and their readiness to assert what they think is most agreeable for the moment" meant that he was often sceptical when native people described the contours of their own land.[10]

And yet lines in the sand, like the beaches upon which they were drawn, were there to be crossed. As the expedition's scientist, Menzies made up to some extent for Vancouver's lack of interest in the cultures of the coast. He was both a more interested and a more perceptive observer of native people. When the expedition first had made contact with Indians off Cape Blanco, he wrote a long description of their physical appearance, clothes, weapons and canoes. Menzies continued to record a good deal of information about the behaviour of the coastal inhabitants, including the occasions when they advanced beyond the lines inscribed by the newcomers. He also made some effort, when time permitted, to understand the Indian languages and was quick to recognize that there were numerous linguistic differences even over short distances.

Menzies was, however, conscious of the limitations of his knowledge and avoided hasty conclusions. Both Menzies and Vancouver were interested in the possibility of population decline among the coast Indians. Large burial sites and deserted villages led to speculation about causes. Sometimes Menzies simply felt that the observed population was "too small for such a fine territory." He thought that perhaps a hunting way of life could not sustain a large population, he wondered about the impact of warfare, and he considered the possibility that In-

FACING PAGE: *The shores on the south side [of the Strait of Juan de Fuca] are composed of low sandy cliffs, falling perpendicularly on beaches of sand or stones.*

About this time a very high conspicuous craggy
mountain, bearing by compass N. 50 E. presented
itself, . . . it was covered with snow; . . . [it was]
discovered in the afternoon by the third lieutenant, and
in compliment to him called by me MOUNT BAKER.

To describe the beauties of this region, will, on some
future occasion, be a very grateful task to the pen of a
skilful panegyrist.

dians had moved to be near the centres of trade. These were all interesting hypotheses, but in the end he had to admit that "they could form no conjecture or opinion on the cause of this apparent depopulation which had not an equal chance of proving fallacious from their circumscribed knowledge of the manners & modes of living of the Natives."[11] It is a pity that more recent scholars have not always emulated Menzies' caution when evaluating the evidence of depopulation in the early contact period.

After spending some time on the coast, even Vancouver acknowledged the limitations on his ability to comprehend coastal cultures. Except at Nootka Sound, which he revisited several times, he did not have sufficient contact with any one group to learn much about them. There were fleeting encounters with groups of Indians who paddled to the vessels and boats or on beaches where Vancouver's men went ashore for brief periods. Like many European observers, Vancouver thought that the people of the northern coast were more attractive and congenial than those farther south.[12] Yet even with his curiosity quickened, there were things that he could not know. He might record what he saw as accurately as possible, but he had little insight. At some places on the northern coast he noticed native women taking an active and even determining role in trade with his men. Vancouver wondered whether this was a matriarchal society but realized that he could not be sure: "The knowledge we obtained of their manners and customs, in our short acquaintance, was however too superficial to establish this or any other fact, that did not admit of ocular demonstration."[13]

Though misunderstanding could easily lead to violence when the representatives of different cultures came together, Vancouver arrived on the coastline determined to avoid conflict with its people. His men were certainly very vulnerable in their little boats, and he wanted them to work in safety, but it was not just a matter of self-interest. He also believed that no Indians should lose their lives because of his presence, and throughout the first and most of the second season, he maintained peaceful relations with the native people. While Vancouver believed that he was the determining factor in avoiding violence, the people of the coast had reasons of their own for tolerating his presence. Vancouver's men were there to explore the coast, but they also traded some furs on the side to make a little profit. At one village at the mouth of the Nimpkish River on the east coast of Vancouver Island, they purchased more than two hundred sea-otter pelts.[14] This was an activity that the native people could understand, particularly if there were an advantage in it for them, and trading undoubtedly helped to smooth the waters. Later, in the north, the tenor of things would change, but, during his early months on the coast, Vancouver's contact with the people was usually cordial, if

FACING PAGE: *I became acquainted, that the first inlet communicated with port Gardner, by a very narrow and intricate channel, which, for a considerable distance, was not forty yards in width, and abounded with rocks above and beneath the surface of the water. These impediments, in addition to the great rapidity and irregularity of the tide, rendered the passage navigable only for boats or vessels of very small burthen.*

superficial. Certainly he quickly realized that charting the coast involved more than hydrography: it also required successful mediation between cultures.

With the survey begun in Puget Sound, Vancouver moved on to what, in retrospect, would be one of the most significant phases of his work. His second major anchorage was Birch Bay on the mainland coast just south of the forty-ninth parallel. From there, the boats were sent north and south. Vancouver and Puget led the excursion northward. They examined Boundary Bay, rounded Point Roberts and passed by the mouth of the Fraser River. Once again, Vancouver chose not to investigate a major river. He concluded that the shoals at the mouth meant that the channels could not be navigated by boats of any size, so he continued on to Burrard Inlet. He was the first European to enter the inner harbour, but, as he was soon to discover, he was not the only mariner in the area. From Burrard Inlet they continued north to Howe Sound and Jervis Inlet before turning back towards *Discovery* in Birch Bay. As they approached Point Grey on their return, Vancouver was startled to see two Spanish vessels riding at anchor.

The *Sutil* and *Mexicana* represented continued Spanish interest in the coast. They were commanded by Dionisio Alcalá Galiano and Cayetano Valdés, who had been sent to examine the waters inside the Strait of Juan de Fuca. Their reconnaissance was an offshoot of the major scientific expedition led by Alejandro Malaspina which had been on the coast the previous summer. Farther north another Spanish expedition under Jacinto Caamaño was investigating the area around Dixon Entrance. Like Vancouver, the Spanish were looking for the northwest passage or, as they more romantically called it, the Strait of Anian. Vancouver was vexed to find that the Spanish were surveying in the Strait of Georgia, which he thought he had to himself. It was even more jarring to learn that a Spanish expedition, under the command of Francisco de Eliza, had been in the strait the previous year. He perhaps took some consolation from the fact that their work was less thorough than his.

In spite of the rivalry between nations, cordial relations were established between the two expeditions meeting on a distant shore. No one with Vancouver spoke Spanish, but Galiano knew some English. Vancouver was informed that Juan Francisco de la Bodega y Quadra, the Spanish representative appointed to settle the terms of the Nootka Sound Convention, was waiting at Nootka to begin negotiations. In the meantime, the coastline beckoned. Vancouver had an inkling that there might be a channel to the north that joined up with the open sea. He and the Spanish commanders decided to pool their information about the area and to continue on together. Vancouver made it clear, however, that international cooperation did not mean that he was prepared to take the word of the Spanish for anything. Valdés surveyed Toba Inlet and, on the way out, met Puget going in. The Spanish officer, who told Puget that he had gone to the end of the inlet, was rather disconcerted when Puget went ahead to check for himself. As thorough as ever, Vancouver explained to the Spanish that, whatever they accomplished, his instructions were still to explore every inlet on the coast.[15]

The company of the Spanish did help to mitigate the dreariness of the coast. Compared to the subdued landscape of the Puget Sound area that reminded him of home, the wild and rugged coast farther north made Vancouver feel alien and ill at ease. While anchored in one place to ride out a violent squall, he wrote that the surroundings presented "as gloomy and dismal an aspect as nature could well be supposed to exhibit, had she not been a little aided by vegetation; which though dull and uninteresting, screened from our sight the dreary rocks and precipices that compose these desolate shores . . . an awful silence pervaded the gloomy forests, whilst animated nature seemed to have deserted the neighboring country." The towering, overpowering coast was relentless and dominating. "Our residence here," wrote Vancouver, "was truly forlorn"; and he named the place Desolation Sound as an expression of his feelings for it.[16]

Vancouver was even more anxious to leave when Johnstone returned from an excursion to the north with firmer evidence of a passage to the open sea. He had found Bute Inlet, and at Arran Rapids the water came through with such force that Johnstone concluded the narrow passage led to a much larger body of water. Having reprovisioned, he immediately set off on another boat trip that took him into Johnstone Strait, which gave him a view of Queen Charlotte Strait. Thus Johnstone was the first European to establish that Vancouver Island was separate from the continental shore. At the same time, Puget had rounded Cape Mudge at the southern tip of Quadra Island and entered Discovery Passage. Here too the

"View in Desolation Sound," monochrome watercolour
by J. Sykes. HYDROGRAPHIC OFFICE, TAUNTON,
VIEW NO. 45

"Village of the Friendly Indians at the entrance of Bute's Canal," sketch by T. Heddington, engraved by J. Landseer. VANCOUVER, A VOYAGE, VOL. I, P. 326

current flowed rapidly from the north, indicating that it led to the open sea. Puget's channel also had the advantage of being large enough for *Discovery* to negotiate.

With a major point of geography to establish, Vancouver doubtless did not consider it unlucky to leave Desolation Sound on Friday 13 July. He parted company with Galiano and Valdés, who did not want to slow Vancouver down. They urged him to proceed as quickly as possible to Nootka Sound where Bodega y Quadra awaited his arrival. But Vancouver had his own schedule to keep. He did not want to arrive at Nootka ahead of *Daedalus*, which was supposed to carry further instructions on the negotiations with the Spanish. As he entered the maze of islands and inlets that separated the large island from the mainland, Vancouver saw little reason to rush his exploration in the interests of diplomacy.

Amongst his discoveries was, once again, the realization that an explorer is not necessarily first on the scene. He visited a village at Cape Mudge which he reckoned to be inhabited by at least three hundred people. Then, a few days up Johnstone Strait, at the mouth of the Nimpkish River, he, Menzies and some officers were guests at a much larger village. They called it Cheslakees' village after the the individual whom they took to be the ranking leader. Though he had left the territory of the Salish Indians and was now among Kwa'kwala-speaking groups, Vancouver was still slow to recognize the cultural diversity of the coast. The issue was somewhat confused by the fact that these people understood the language spoken at Nootka Sound. Cheslakees also acknowledged the power, though not necessarily the hegemony, of Maquinna. The Nimpkish River people had a long-standing trading relationship with the people on the other side of the island at Nootka, who acted as middlemen between the Nimpkish and the maritime fur traders. This was their first direct contact with Europeans, but they had already profited from the trade in furs. Vancouver noticed that they were familiar with European goods and was particularly concerned about the number of firearms in the village. They were, thought Vancouver, "well versed in the principles of trade," and Menzies commented that the price of sea-otter furs had gone up by two hundred per cent since he was last on the coast.[17]

Leaving Cheslakees' village, they continued northward. Though their major objective was to find the open sea, side issues were still investigated. Broughton was sent in *Chatham* to probe Knight Inlet. If the cultural differences on the coast remained unclear, the geographical variety could not be ignored. In contrast to the low-lying shore of Vancouver Island, men and ships were rendered insignificant by the vertical mountainsides that knifed into the water beside them in the mainland inlets. Vancouver reported that the shore of Knight Inlet was

"View of Indian Village on Cape Mudge, Gulf of Georgia," monochrome watercolour by *J. Sykes.*
HYDROGRAPHIC OFFICE, TAUNTON, VIEW NO. 44

"Cheslakee's Village in Johnstone's Straits," sketch by
J. Sykes, engraved by J. Landseer. VANCOUVER, A
VOYAGE, VOL. I, P. 346

"The Discovery on the Rocks in Queen Charlotte's Sound," sketch by Z. Mudge, engraved by B. T. Pouncy. VANCOUVER, *A VOYAGE,* VOL. I, P. 364

*"View of Woody Point, on the Island of Quadra &
Vancouver (Vancouver Island)...," monochrome
watercolour by J. Sykes.* HYDROGRAPHIC OFFICE,
TAUNTON, VIEW NO. 46

FACING PAGE: *Mr. Broughton informed me, that the
part of the coast he had been directed to explore,
consisted of an archipelago of islands lying before an
extensive arm of the sea stretching in a variety of
branches between the N.W. north, and N.N.E. Its
extent in the first direction was the most capacious, and
presented an unbounded horizon.*

"formed by high stupendous mountains rising almost perpendicularly from the water's edge. The dissolving snow on their summits produced many cataracts that fell with great impetuosity down their barren rugged sides. The fresh water that thus descended gave a pale white hue to the channel."[18]

The land was intimidating and the sea would soon assert its power. The survey had gone without major mishap through the summer, perhaps lulling them to the dangers of the work, but sailing an uncharted coast was still a risky business. One false move could bring complete disaster. They had passed with comparative ease through the treacherous Seymour Narrows and Johnstone Strait and were now out in the more open waters of Queen Charlotte Strait. Yet there were still reefs and shoals to negotiate, and, when the fog descended, they were at the mercy of the currents. On the afternoon of 6 August the fog cleared enough for Vancouver to see a channel ahead. It was littered with rocks and islets, but there was no better prospect in view, so he decided to go ahead. *Discovery* moved gingerly forward in a light breeze. Then, at about four in the afternoon, with the sounds of wrenching and tearing, she grounded on a submerged reef.

Going aground on an ebbing tide "was alarming in the highest degree." The anchor did not hold, so all they could do was shore up the vessel with masts and spars, jettison part of the load to make her lighter, and hope for the best. As the tide continued to fall, *Discovery* was swung over on her starboard side and the water came within inches of surging over the rail and swamping her. Fortunately there was no swell, or they would certainly have been lost. It was a tense and agonizing evening. By nine o'clock the bow of the ship was in only three feet of water. Then, inevitably, the tide began to turn, and gradually *Discovery* came upright. They floated her off at two in the morning, and miraculously she was virtually unscathed. The mishap was nevertheless a telling reminder of just how tenuous their presence on the coast was. And the lesson was reinforced when *Chatham* went aground the following evening. Once again they were lucky, as

Chatham escaped without major damage. Whidbey was sent ahead to find a safe passage out, and both vessels were finally extricated from a dangerous situation.[19]

Having sailed up the east coast of what was now clearly a large island, Vancouver was still not in a hurry to get to Nootka Sound. He had missed Seymour and Belize inlets because of their particularly narrow entranceways, but there were many more inlets to investigate. The two ships anchored in Safety Cove on the east shore of Calvert Island, and the boat crews went to work again. Smith Sound, Rivers Inlet and Burke Channel were all examined and added to the chart.

Then, by mid-August, Vancouver was ready to call it quits for the season. The weather had taken a turn for the worse, adding to the discomfort of the boat crews, who had already done a long summer of backbreaking work. And a British trading vessel had brought news that *Daedalus* was waiting at Nootka Sound. Vancouver also learned that three of the storeship's crew, the commander James Hergest and the astronomer William Gooch, along with a seaman, had been killed by Hawaiians at Waimea Bay on Oahu. The losses were particularly depressing for Vancouver as Hergest was a close friend and Gooch's expertise would have helped to speed up the surveys. With no reason to further delay his arrival at Nootka, he concluded the work a month early. The expedition took its leave "of these northern solitary regions, whose broken appearance presented a prospect of abundant employment for the ensuing season."[20] They sailed around the northern tip of Vancouver Island and down its west coast to Nootka Sound.

When he dropped anchor in Friendly Cove, Vancouver became the first European to circle Vancouver Island, if one adds together the sections covered with Cook and those sailed in 1792. Galiano and Valdés arrived at Nootka a few days later to complete the first continuous circumnavigation of what was then called Vancouver and Quadra Island in recognition of the joint effort. In his meticulous way, Vancouver had also mapped the west coast of North America between 39° and 52° north latitude. His careful examination of the Strait of Juan de Fuca and its adjacent waterways had eliminated one potential source of the mythical passage through the continent. Long stretches of coast awaited to the north, but already in one summer he had done more to chart the shoreline than any other single explorer.

With all this accomplished in just four months, he now turned from the geographic to the diplomatic side of his mission. Here too he was careful to a fault. The particular point at issue at Nootka Sound in August 1792 was the amount of land to be handed over by the Spanish representative to the British. Vancouver had assumed that clear instructions on the point would arrive with *Daedalus*. He was disappointed when all he received was more generalities from London, along

FACING PAGE: *The shoal having forced us nearly into the middle of the gulf, we stood over to its western side, in order to land for the night, and to cook our provisions for the ensuing day, . . . it was with much difficulty we were enabled to land on the steep rugged rocks that compose the coast.*

"A View of Friendly Cove in Nootka Sound, A to B comprising the territories, districts, & parcels of land, offered to be ceded by Sigr. Quadra, on the part of the Court of Spain To Geo. Vancouver Esqr., on the part of His Britannic Majesty, the rest remaining the property of the Court of Spain," pen and ink with monochrome watercolour by H. Humphrys. PUBLIC RECORD OFFICE, LONDON, MFQ 127

with a copy of a letter from Count Floridablanca, the Spanish foreign minister, instructing the commandant at Nootka to surrender those lands that had been in the hands of British subjects in April 1789. This information told Vancouver nothing that he did not already know. He was therefore left in a very difficult position by his own government and was not one to improvise on what he saw as a crucial matter. Bodega y Quadra, in the meantime, had been checking the facts during the summer when Nootka was visited by a number of traders who had also been there in 1789. Questioned by Bodega, they denied that Meares had purchased land from Maquinna and claimed that he had built only a very rudimentary dwelling. Accordingly, the Spaniard was prepared to hand over only a tiny slip of land in one corner of Friendly Cove where Meares had erected his "house." This "small pittance of rocks and sandy beach" was much less than Vancouver was willing to accept.[21] There was an inconclusive exchange of letters between the two, and they finally agreed to submit the matter back to London and Madrid. Vancouver sent a detailed account of the negotiations to Britain, together with a drawing by Henry Humphrys that clearly indicated the tiny piece of land that Bodega was prepared to return.

The diplomatic impasse did not prevent the development of cordial personal relations between Vancouver and Bodega. They wined and dined each other and merrily blazed away with mutual thirteen-gun salutes until the British expedition, at least, was short of ammunition. All this heartiness and good will may have limited Vancouver's ability to take a hard line with Bodega. He believed that he had "uniformly persisted in my determination of strictly adhering to the line of my duty," yet he was also defensive about his painfully cautious approach to diplomacy and hoped that he would not be liable to censure. At least one commentator in Britain, Philip Stephens, the secretary of the Admiralty, regretted that Vancouver had not settled on Bodega's terms. He argued that the amount of land was less important than the preservation of national honour by some kind of restitution.[22] It was probably unreasonable to expect Vancouver, whose profession was to delineate specific stretches of shoreline in meticulous detail, to carry off grand gestures of international diplomacy.

Europeans often assumed, of course, that diplomacy was a white man's game. Thus Vancouver and Bodega, as the representatives of Britain and Spain, haggled over land at Nootka as if they owned the place. Neither recognized that there was a third player who had more power and authority in Nootka Sound than the two of them put together. As the ranking native leader at Nootka Sound, Maquinna, no less than Vancouver and Bodega, asserted his role as an international diplomat. He denied that he had ever "sold" land to Meares, though he may well have granted the British trader temporary use of a small part of his territory.

Maquinna had come to power as a traditional leader, but his role also had changed as a result of the European presence on the coast. He had probably assumed his position of leadership on the death of his father in 1778, becoming the ranking individual among a group who lived on the west side of Nootka Sound. They had a winter village at the head of Tahsis Inlet, and Yuquot, at the opening of the sound, was one of their summer dwelling places. Maquinna was a striking and forceful individual. John Meares described him as "of a middle size, but extremely well made, and possessing a countenance that was formed to interest all who saw him."[23] He led his people through the early years of the maritime fur trade, using their strategic location to control the exchange of goods in the Nootka area. He became very wealthy and therefore very powerful through his ability to manipulate the fur trade. At the same time, he recognized that the growing international rivalry over Nootka Sound had the potential to interrupt the trade and undermine his leadership. When Martínez began arresting British vessels in 1789, Maquinna and his people knew that if traders stopped coming to Nootka they would be the first to suffer. Maquinna's close relative, Callicum, paddled out to berate the Spanish and was shot dead by a seaman. The growing tension threatened to diminish Maquinna's prestige in his own community, so he

Interior of Maquinna's house at Tahsis, sketch by José María Vasquez from a sketch by Atanasío Echeverría.
ARCHIVO GENERAL Y BIBLIOTECA, MINISTERIO DE ASUNTOS EXTERIORES, MADRID

"View of the Entrance into Nootka Sound...,"
monochrome watercolour by J. Sykes.
HYDROGRAPHIC OFFICE, TAUNTON, VIEW NO. 48

left Nootka Sound for a time to live with another powerful leader, Wickaninnish, at Clayoquot Sound. He later returned to Nootka, but, as long as the Spanish were in possession of Yuquot, he did not live there. The next few years were uneasy ones for the native leader, both in his relations with Europeans and among his own people.

When Vancouver arrived at Nootka Sound, his relations with Maquinna did not get off to a good start. The native leader tried to come aboard *Discovery*, but was prevented by the deck officer, who did not realize who he was. Fortunately the gaffe in protocol was smoothed over by Bodega, who had already established a rapport with Maquinna. A few days later both commanders visited Maquinna's village. They were served a meal followed by dancing and ceremonial. Vancouver was unmoved by the ritual of the occasion, commenting when Maquinna danced in a mask that it was "ridiculously laughable." Menzies took native observances more seriously, but his commander remained unimpressed by the customs of the people and the status of their leader. When Maquinna and his wives made a return visit to *Discovery*, Vancouver dismissed them "as the most consummate beggars I had ever seen." As Vancouver left Nootka Sound, Maquinna declared that he was sorry to see the British leave and asked for some of them to stay behind to protect the local people from harassment by other Europeans. Vancouver thought that the native leader was merely trying to ingratiate himself through flattery and remarked, "Very little dependence... is to be placed in the truth or sincerity of such declarations."[24] While Vancouver did not accept Maquinna as an individual of consequence, others certainly did.

On the Northwest Coast a leader had a reciprocal relationship with his people. Rank was achieved through lineage, but leadership was maintained by providing for others. By 1789, Maquinna's wealth, and therefore that of his people, had become closely tied to the presence of European traders. So the native leader had an interest in re-establishing cordial relations with the newcomers. In the summer of 1792 matters improved somewhat when he renewed friendly contact with the Spanish through the affable Bodega. Then Vancouver arrived, representing the nation that intended to take over Nootka from the Spanish. As the leader with the most at stake at the local level, Maquinna had to have a seat at the table for the new round of diplomacy. The initial rebuff at the rail of *Discovery* must have been devastating. But the arrival of both European commanders at his village and their acceptance of his hospitality provided an important boost to his prestige. In indigenous terms, they were his guests receiving his bounty and thereby were affirming his pre-eminence. Vancouver saw that Maquinna's "pride was not a little indulged by our shewing him this attention," but the British commander had no

"View of Monterrey," monochrome watercolour by J. Sykes. HYDROGRAPHIC OFFICE, TAUNTON, VIEW NO. 62

idea that, at another level, he was also a pawn in the internal politics of Nootka Sound.[25]

Without having reached agreement with Bodega or appreciating the importance of Maquinna, Vancouver left Nootka Sound on 12 October 1792 and sailed south towards warmer weather. Not that surveying was quite over for the season. Whidbey investigated Gray's Harbor and Broughton managed to get *Chatham* over the treacherous bar of the Columbia River to chart its lower reaches. He rowed the boats about one hundred miles upstream to Point Vancouver and took formal possession of the area for Great Britain. In the meantime *Discovery* had a long and laborious passage towards San Francisco Bay. Once he reached his initial landfall at Point Cabrillo, Vancouver began to survey the coast southward to the extent that conditions permitted. *Discovery* was the first non-Spanish vessel to visit San Francisco Bay when she sailed through the Golden Gate on 14 November. After a ten-day stay, Vancouver moved on to Monterey. At both Spanish settlements, largely because of the personal influence of Bodega y Quadra, the British expedition was received with open-handed hospitality. Vancouver and his officers dined at Spanish tables, made frequent excursions by horseback into the surrounding countryside, and were generously received at the Spanish missions. Vancouver wrote extensive dispatches both on his survey of the coast and his negotiations at Nootka Sound to send to Britain with Broughton, who sailed as far as San Blas with Bodega. With the reports written and the vessels replenished, he left to spend the rest of the winter in Hawaii.

"The Mission of St. Carlos near Monterrey," monochrome watercolour by J. Sykes. HYDROGRAPHIC OFFICE, TAUNTON, VIEW NO. 64

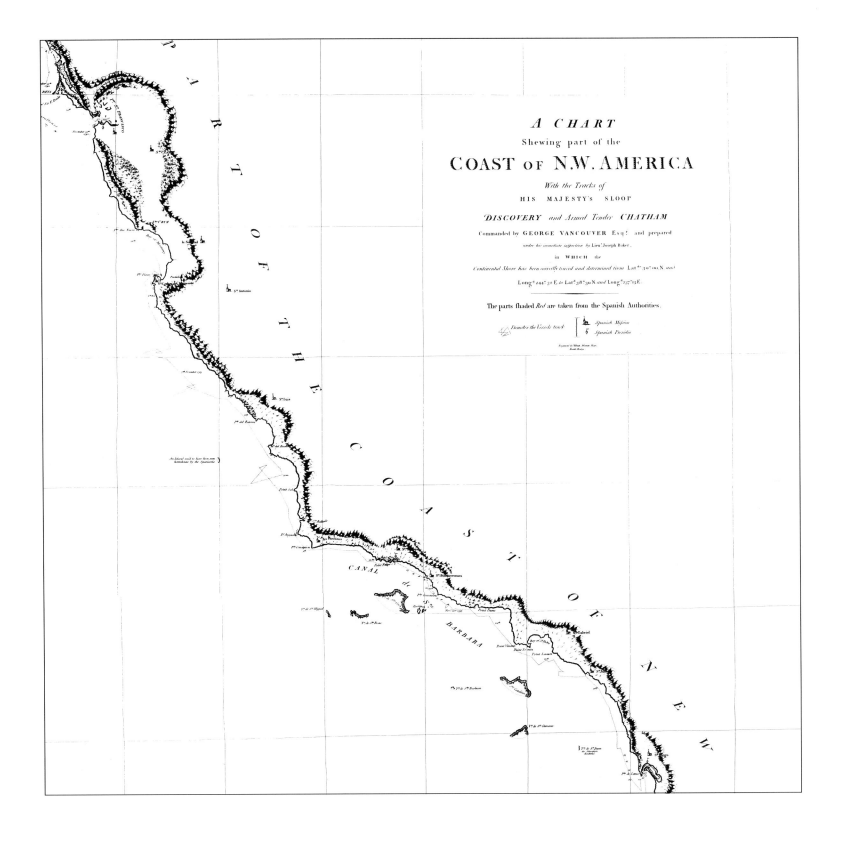

A CHART

Shewing part of the

COAST of N.W. AMERICA

With the Tracks of

HIS MAJESTY'S SLOOP

DISCOVERY and Armed Tender CHATHAM

Commanded by GEORGE VANCOUVER Esq.r and prepared

under his immediate inspection by Lieu.t Joseph Baker.

in WHICH the

Continental Shore has been correctly traced and determined from Lat.de 30°.00.N. and

Long.d 244°.32.E. to Lat.d 38°.30.N. and Long.d 237°.15.E.

The parts shaded Red are taken from the Spanish Authorities.

Denotes the Vessels track   Spanish Mission   Spanish Presidio

"The Presidio of Monterrey," monochrome watercolour by J. Sykes. HYDROGRAPHIC OFFICE, TAUNTON, VIEW NO. 63

They sighted Cape Kumukahi, the eastern point of Hawaii, on 12 February 1793 and remained in Hawaiian waters until the end of March. Vancouver continued to be rather more interested in Hawaii than the Northwest Coast. His lively and engaged accounts of both the islands and the people contrast with his routine and often sombre commentary on the coast. Of course, Vancouver came to Hawaii so that his vessels could be refitted and his men could relax in more congenial surroundings after the hard grind on the northern coast, so he was bound to feel more at ease. Yet even here there was work to be done. As well as charting some sections of Hawaiian coastline for the first time, Vancouver had two other objectives in mind. The first was to try to bring peace between the warring factions on the various islands, and the second was to arrange some kind of cession of the Hawaiian Islands to Great Britain.

Such diplomacy seemed feasible to Vancouver because, in contrast to his disdain for Maquinna, he recognized the strength and authority of Hawaiian leaders. On the Northwest Coast, particularly in the south, Vancouver and his men often could not tell who were the leaders. There were chiefs by name, but they seemed to have no authority, and there was no subordination on the part of the people. It was very difficult, from a European perspective, to figure out the indigenous political system.[26] But they experienced no such confusion in Hawaii, where leadership was more formalized than in Northwest Coast societies. Hawaiian chiefs had absolute power over their people. Moreover, Vancouver was in Hawaii at a time when a few strongmen were contending for control over the whole island chain.[27] All of these features of Hawaiian power and politics were readily appreciated by Europeans. Indeed, outsiders, and particularly their weapons, played some role in these dynastic wars. Vancouver deplored the trade in guns and was distressed by the destruction caused by the endless conflict. Because he believed "that a continuation of such commotions would soon desolate these islands," he refused to trade firearms and was careful not to provide material assistance to any one side in the struggle.[28] Not that Vancouver's motives were entirely altruistic. He wanted to bring peace to the islands so that the people could return to producing the food supplies so essential to traders coming to and from the Northwest Coast.

Vancouver discussed the possibility of peace first with Kamehameha, who by 1793 controlled the Island of Hawaii. He then tried to bring Kamehameha and his chief rival, Kahekili, who held sway over the islands to the leeward of Hawaii, together for peace negotiations. After years of fighting, neither side trusted the other enough to arrange a meeting. For his part, Kamehameha was engaged in a series of wars that, within two years, would establish his hegemony over all the Hawaiian Islands except Kauai. He was rather more interested in using Vancouver's presence to strengthen his hand in the final battle than in bringing about a peaceful settlement. Once again, Vancouver was over his head in diplomatic waters, and he failed to bring the warfare to an end. He did raise the question of ceding the islands to Britain with Kamehameha, without getting a definitive answer. But he would broach that question again the following year.

Vancouver had two other matters to deal with before leaving the Hawaiian Islands. First, he was determined to find and punish those responsible for killing Hergest and Gooch. During a brief stay at Waikiki, three men alleged to be involved in the murders were brought to Vancouver's ship, and they were "tried" and executed. The evidence of their guilt was scarcely conclusive, and it is likely that the three unfortunates were served up by Hawaiian chiefs to placate Vancouver. It also became clear that Hergest's own ill-considered behaviour had been largely responsible for the deaths at Waimea the previous year.[29] Vancouver's final task was to return home two Hawaiian women who had been taken to Nootka Sound on a fur-trading vessel. He left them at his final port of call on Kauai. Once this was done, "we hauled our wind to the north-west, and with all sails set, we bade adieu to the Sandwich Islands for the present, and made the best of our way towards Nootka."[30]

FACING PAGE, LEFT AND RIGHT: *On due consideration of all the circumstances . . . I became thoroughly convinced, that our boats alone could enable us to acquire any correct or satisfactory information respecting this broken country.*

In this dreary and comfortless region, it was no inconsiderable piece of good fortune to find a little cove in which we could take shelter, . . . as we had scarcely finished our examination when the wind became excessively boisterous from the southward, attended with heavy squalls and torrents of rain.

Into the Labyrinth

UNFORTUNATELY, "THE BEST OF OUR WAY" WAS LONG AND ARDUOUS, and it was a foretaste of things to come during the second season on the coast. Gloomy weather and adverse winds meant that it took four weeks to sail from Hawaii to the Northwest Coast. To make matters worse, *Discovery* had a leak in her bow which, although above the waterline, let in more than a foot of water an hour in heavy seas and required constant bailing. They reached the coast near Cape Mendocino and anchored in Trinidad Harbor. After a brief pause they pressed north again, sailing against the wind. Vancouver did not reach Nootka until late in May, only to find that *Chatham* had already been and gone to resume the survey. He observed that over the winter the Spanish under Salvador Fidalgo had built new fortifications on San Miguel Island at one end of Friendly Cove. While Vancouver did not set much store by this fort, others thought that it hardly indicated the Spanish intended to vacate Nootka. *Discovery* was also visited by Maquinna, who announced that his daughter had been betrothed to the eldest son of Wickaninnish. Maquinna was still consolidating his position. Vancouver did not dally at Nootka, for he was eager to move on, as the long passage from Hawaii had already taken a month out of his survey time on the coast. He left after three days to meet up with *Chatham* in Burke Channel, and they anchored together in Restoration Cove (now Restoration Bay).

Then they simply began where they had left off. By now Vancouver knew that he would have to be as relentless as the tide—exploring every opening, every weakness in the coast's defences—if the survey were to be complete. And so the routine was the same as last year. An anchorage was found where there was wood and fresh water so that spruce beer could be brewed as a preventive for scurvy. Whenever possible, as much fresh food as the coast would provide was

FACING PAGE: *This promontory, after my first lieutenant, . . . obtained the name of* POINT MUDGE. . . . *On point Mudge was a very large village of the natives. . . . Round point Mudge, at a distance of about half a mile, is a ledge of sunken rocks; these are, however, easily avoided by the weeds which they produce.*

gathered. Sometimes the shore was bountiful. They traded with the native people or fished for salmon and halibut, and, in the north, they gathered oolichan, which "proved to be the most delicate eating." As well as seafood, "our sportsmen added some ducks, geese, and other aquatic birds; . . . so that with different sorts of berries which the shores produced, the tables of the officers were by no means ill supplied. The wild fowl were not obtained in such numbers as to serve the ship's company," but, where they were available, "of the fish and fruit they always had a due proportion."[1] Some anchorages were not so fruitful. They were glad to leave one such place in Princess Royal Channel where "neither the sea nor the shores afforded us the smallest refreshment." As they departed, some crew members christened it "Starve-Gut Cove."[2] Fortunately the coast was usually more hospitable. At most anchorages, while supplies were replenished, repairs were made to the vessels. And usually the observatory was set up on shore so that astronomical observations could fix their exact location.

From each of these focal points, the boat crews were sent out into the surrounding area to continue the survey. Up each of the long, sinuous inlets they laboured, and down again after they reached the end and found, as they rather expected, that it did not penetrate the mountains. They would often be away from the vessel for more than two weeks, and when they returned to base, another small segment of coastline could be added to the charts. In this way they slowly unravelled the tangled skein of inlets and islands that make up the coast between Vancouver Island and the Alaska panhandle.

Some improvements were made to conditions in the boats as a result of the experience of the previous season. Extra rations were provided so that the crews could have two hot meals a day, and "in consequence of their being much exposed to the prevailing inclement weather, an additional quantity of spirits" was added to the supplies "to be used at the discretion of the officer commanding each party."[3] The boats were also provided with canvas awnings to protect the men from wind and rain, as well as a tent to sleep in at night. Each crew member had gear stashed away in a canvas bag so that he did not have to suffer the discomfort of wet clothes. The seamen were no doubt grateful for these changes, but they still faced long, exhausting days at the oars. And a soft word like "inclement" hardly described the weather that summer. More often than not it was raging and raining, or damp and dreary.

Vancouver himself led only two boat excursions during the summer of 1793, a sign that his health was deteriorating. The rest were commanded by Whidbey or Johnstone. Vancouver remained largely unmoved by the grandeur of the coast, which he still found more depressing than uplifting. "The appearance of the country we had passed by," he noted on his first boat trip, "varied in no respect from what has already been frequently described." He did experience a couple of moments of awe. In Cascade Inlet off Dean Channel, he was impressed by the waterfalls that came crashing down beside him: "These were extremely grand, and by much the largest and most tremendous of any we had ever beheld." Then, farther north on his second boat trip, in Behm Canal, he came upon a "remarkable rock" standing out in the middle of the channel. At its base the circumference was about fifty yards, and it rose perpendicular to, he estimated, a height of upwards of two hundred and fifty feet. Since it reminded him of the familiar lighthouse off Plymouth, he named it "the New Eddystone." By and large, however, the coast was a "dreary and uninteresting" place. Even Restoration Cove, the first anchorage of the summer, was named for the anniversary of the restoration of Charles II in 1660 and not because it provided Vancouver with a restoration of spirits. He continued to take a professional surveyor's view of the coastline. "This uninteresting region afforded nothing further worthy of notice," he wrote, "excepting the soundings, the dimensions of the cove, and the very few astronomical and nautical observations, that, under the unfavourable circumstances of the weather, could be procured."[4]

Early in the summer, he sometimes took a more lively interest in the native people of the coast, the good will perhaps lingering on from his sojourn in Hawaii. At Trinidad Harbor, just as he had reached the coast again, he encountered a small group of Yurok Indians, whom he described in uncharacteristic detail. Now, on the middle coast, among the Bella Coola and their Heiltsuk-speaking neighbours, he even had some positive things to say. He recognized that they spoke a different language from the people at Nootka Sound, and, like many other early visitors to the coast, he thought them "to be a much finer race of men than those further south." In fact, he added, they rather resembled northern Europeans. Not that he got carried away on the point. He soon went on to note that "the difference however appeared less conspicuous, when they were seen in greater numbers, probably owing to our having become more familiar with their persons." He and most of his crew were repulsed by the labret, a lip ornament that they observed high-ranking women wearing. Vancouver described it as "a species of deformity, and an instance of human absurdity, that would scarcely be credited without ocular proof." Yet these people had fine qualities, and, for once, Vancouver was at ease with pointing them out. Later that summer, among other groups farther north, he would have cause to revise his views somewhat, but these people "appeared to be civil, good-humoured, and friendly." And when they came to trade furs, they were clearly "well versed in commerce."[5]

"View of The New Eddystone a remarkable Rock in Bhering (Behm) Canal," watercolour over pencil by J. *Sykes.* BANCROFT LIBRARY, BERKELEY, ROBERT B. HONEYMAN COLLECTION, NO. 596

"The New Eddystone, in Bhem's Canal," sketch by J.
Sykes, engraved by B. T. Pouncy. VANCOUVER, A
VOYAGE, VOL. II, P. 352

The native people of the coast would be profoundly affected by what one scholar has called a historic "near miss" during Vancouver's first boat excursion of the season.[6] On the night of 4 June 1793, his crew rested near the mouth of a tiny notch called Elcho Harbour in Dean Channel. The next day they examined the small inlet before proceeding down the channel, leaving the spot that another explorer, coming by land from the opposite direction, would reach a few weeks later. The North West Company explorer Alexander Mackenzie had left Fort Chipewyan in the Athabaska country in October 1792, wintered over at the junction of the Peace and Smoky rivers, and set out in May 1793 on a journey towards the Pacific Ocean. Mackenzie drove his men hard and travelled fast. He reached tidewater at Bentinck Arm on 20 July, and two days later, on 22 July 1793, he wrote the terse inscription "Alexander Mackenzie, from Canada, by land" on a rock on the eastern side of the entrance to Elcho Harbour. He was standing where Vancouver had been just six weeks earlier. The Indians described to Mackenzie how Vancouver had left his ship off to the southwest and come to their village in a small boat.[7] The two Europeans had missed each other, but, though neither they nor the native people yet realized the significance of these events, the connection between sea and land had been made.

Vancouver and Mackenzie represented two lines of approach to the coast. At the same time that navigators and traders were opening up lines of commerce from the sea, other explorers were coming in from the land. By the second half of the eighteenth century, two rival fur-trading interests, one out of Montreal and the other out of Hudson Bay, were expanding westward across the continent. They, too, were looking for a northwest passage: a trade route that would take them out to the Pacific and thence to the Orient. In 1778, the same year that Cook was on the coast, Peter Pond crossed Methye Portage into the Athabaska country. Returning to that rich fur-bearing area several times through the 1780s, Pond convinced himself that a river connected Great Slave Lake with Cook's River, as it was then called on the maps, on the Alaskan coast. Now, just as Cook's student was testing geographical theory by sea, a protégé of Pond was exploring the details by land. Alexander Mackenzie had already followed the Mackenzie River to its mouth, but found that it emptied into the Arctic Ocean rather than the Pacific. On his second expedition he found a way across the sea of mountains and became the first European to cross North America. But the real lay of the land did not conform to theory, and Mackenzie had not discovered an easy trade route to the sea.

Not knowing that he had just missed the landward explorer, Vancouver pressed on with his painstaking search. The vessels were moved up the coast

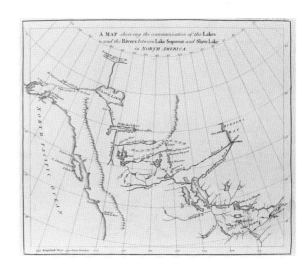

"A Map shewing the communication of the Lakes and the Rivers between Lake Superior and Slave Lake in North America," by Peter Pond, Gentleman's Magazine, *March 1790.* COURTESY JAMES P. RONDA

from anchorage to anchorage, seven in all that season, and at each one the boats fanned out to check out another piece of coastline. In and out of coves and channels, they gradually worked their way northward. Vancouver was sceptical about the existence of any major waterway through the continent, but every inlet had to be investigated, just in case it proved to be the entrance to the northwest passage. Mostly the work must have seemed arduous rather than dangerous, yet occasionally tragedy struck to remind them of the risks that they were running on a daily basis.

On one of his early excursions of the season, James Johnstone led a boat crew up the length of Mathieson Channel. On the morning of 15 June they stopped to have breakfast near the head of the inlet, and, as they had so often done before, some of the crew roasted and ate mussels they gathered on the shore. Within a short time some of the seaman were seized with paralysis as well as becoming sick and giddy. They tried to sweat the poison out of their bodies by rowing furiously, but when they landed for lunch, one man named John Carter died where he lay on the beach. The others affected were then persuaded to drink copious amounts of warm water to induce vomiting, and their lives were saved, though they were ill for a couple of weeks. It seemed that only some of the mussels—those gathered from the sand rather than from the rocks—were toxic, suggesting that a poison was in the water. The fact that they ate the shellfish at breakfast, on empty stomachs, also made the symptoms more severe. The men were probably suffering from a paralytic shellfish poison that is sometimes called red tide, because the toxic organism in high concentrations can colour the water red. There had been another incident the previous summer when some members of a boat crew led by Thomas Manby had become ill from eating shellfish. Manby had them drink an emetic and they survived, but this time the expedition was not so lucky.[8] With great sadness, Vancouver named the burial place of their lost comrade Carter's Bay and the fatal spot where the mussels had been eaten Poison Cove.[9] Yet, incredibly, John Carter was only one of two crew members lost during the three seasons of surveying on the coast.

The death toll among native people as a consequence of Vancouver's presence was somewhat higher. He and his men had had generally peaceful, if occasionally strained, relations with the native groups on the southern coast. Farther north, among the northern Tsimshian and Tlingit, the tenor of things seemed to change. In Observatory Inlet the expedition anchored in Salmon Cove, so named because they acquired large numbers of salmon from a group of Indians who were catching them in a spawning stream. From there, Vancouver led his second boat excursion of the season. At the entrance to Portland Canal, a small group of native

"Salmon Cove. Observatory Inlet," sketch by T. Heddington, engraved by J. Fittler. VANCOUVER, A *VOYAGE,* VOL. II, P. 333

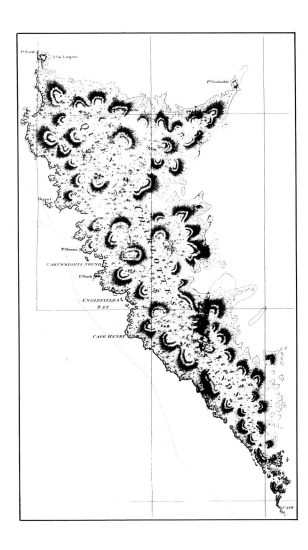

FACING PAGE: *To the south of the village a valley extended, apparently to a considerable distance, in a south-westerly direction. Through it a very fine stream of fresh water emptied itself into the sea. . . . The Ty-eie, or chief of the village, paid us an early visit, and received from me some presents which highly delighted him. I understood his name to be* Cheslakees.

people approached in two canoes. Initial offers to trade did not go smoothly, and they seemed to be preparing their weapons. It was not clear whether they intended to attack or were merely preparing to defend themselves, and, in the event, violence was avoided. But the incident should have warned them that tense situations could easily get out of hand.

Several days later there was a more serious incident. Rowing down Behm Canal on the west side of Revillagigedo Island, they were once again approached by some Tlingit who seemed friendly enough. Vancouver went inshore in a pinnace and landed to take some angles to determine the trend of the shoreline. He left Puget offshore in the launch. Having taken his readings, Vancouver returned to his pinnace. With Indians pressing around on all sides, he became concerned and ordered a quick retreat. They got the pinnace out onto the water but were immediately surrounded by Indians threatening violence and intent on plunder. Puget was too far off to offer immediate help, so Vancouver tried to calm the situation. Each time he seemed to pacify one group of Indians, a new wave of hostility surged from another quarter. Spear thrusts seriously wounded two seamen and a number of muskets were stolen from the boat. Suddenly, the situation was out of control, and it looked as though they would be overwhelmed. Puget had now drawn in close enough to be within gunshot range. Without much hope that they could extricate themselves, Vancouver gave the order to fire on the Indians. To his surprise, the assailants immediately retreated, heading for the shore and then up into the high rocks. Perhaps as many as twelve were killed while others were injured.[10]

Vancouver had come very close to losing his life on a remote shoreline. If, in that wild moment, he thought of Cook, he does not appear to have committed the recollection to paper. He did reflect on the incident afterward, wondering if they had inadvertently given offence to the Tlingit. He did not think they had, so he was more inclined to the view that the Indians were trying to take revenge for some previous insult from another European. Maritime fur traders had already been in the area, and the Tlingit indicated that they had been given defective firearms that sometimes blew up in their faces. Vancouver once again deplored the trade in guns and the havoc that they created. In the end, however, he had to admit that the conflict with the Tlingit had erupted because he and his men had relaxed their guard. As he put it, "that attentive wariness which had been the first object of my concern on coming among these rude nations, had latterly been much neglected."[11]

If the explorers were to avoid further violence, they would have to be more careful. Later, a boat party led by Whidbey was also in Behm Canal when they

came upon a Tlingit group beckoning them ashore. The Indians each laid a bit of white wool on the rocks which was taken as a sign of peace. Some of Whidbey's party thought that these were the same Indians who had attacked Vancouver and now were appealing for forgiveness. Still, Whidbey decided that it was too risky to land and passed by. On another occasion, when Johnstone was in command of the boats, a large group in about twenty canoes suddenly appeared around a headland. This time the Indians were kept away from the boats with warning shots. By keeping their distance, they were able to avoid further bloodshed, but Vancouver still felt that the earlier killings had marred his record on the coast. He had hoped to complete the survey without firing a single shot in anger and was disturbed that he had failed.

There were other concerns as well. At the end of his own boat trip, Vancouver returned to *Discovery* in mid-August after twenty-three days under oars. His crew had rowed upwards of seven hundred miles, but he had advanced the survey of the continental coastline not more than sixty miles: "Such were the perplexing, tedious, and laborious means by which alone we were enabled by degrees to trace the north-western limits of the American continent."[12] As it turned out, it was the last major boat expedition that Vancouver would lead. The boat trip took a great deal out of him, and his health was growing worse. Still he pressed on, examining the waters around Clarence Strait before moving up into Sumner Strait. Looking for a safe haven, he anchored in a sheltered cove on the northern tip of Prince of Wales Island. No sooner were the sails furled than a furious storm blew up and raged through the night. Vancouver was certain that, if they had not found refuge, the ships would have been wrecked, and he named the place Port Protection.

When the weather subsided, the final surveying sorties of the season were sent out. Whidbey led a boat party down the western shore of Sumner Strait to its opening to the sea but at that point decided not to turn northward to examine the open coast. Johnstone had made two errors that led the crews to believe they were tracing the continental shore rather than the coast of Kupreanof and Kuiu islands. Approaching the shoals and mud at the wide, shallow estuary of the Stikine River, he had not probed the narrow passage called Dry Strait that separates Kupreanof Island from the mainland. A couple of weeks later he had missed Keku Strait that runs through to Frederick Sound between Kupreanof and Kuiu islands. These two points would have to be sorted out next season. But now it was the third week of September, the coast was working up for winter, and storms were lashing in from the Pacific. On his way back to the vessels, Whidbey had stopped overnight in a cove that did not provide as much shelter as he expected. A heavy

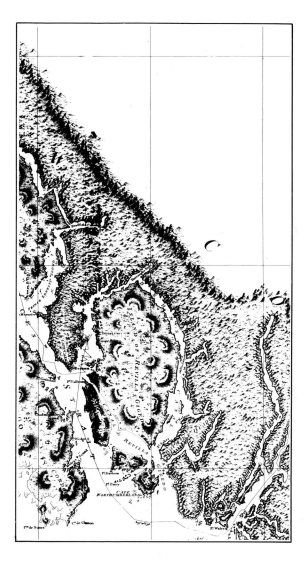

FACING PAGE: *The shores either constituted impenetrable forests, produced from the fissures of a rugged rocky country, or were formed by stupendous barren precipices, rising perpendicularly from the water to an immense height.*

"View from the anchorage of the head of Port Protection, NW Coast of America," monochrome watercolour by J. Sykes. HYDROGRAPHIC OFFICE, TAUNTON, VIEW NO. 40

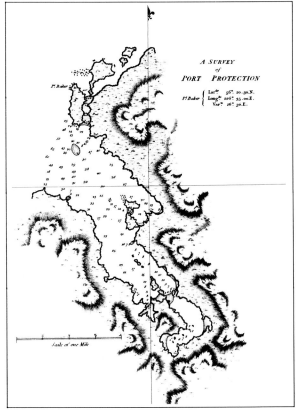

"View of Cape St. James, the South Point of Queen Charlotte's Islands . . . ," monochrome watercolour by J. Sykes. HYDROGRAPHIC OFFICE, TAUNTON, VIEW NO. 43

swell rolled in from the south and nearly smashed his boats against the rocky shore. The boat work was getting very risky, and, for now, Vancouver had had enough: "The boisterous state of the weather, the advanced season of the year, and the approach of long dreary nights, left me in no doubt concerning the measures that ought to be now adopted."[13]

Vancouver decided to conclude the work for the season. He was not entirely happy with the progress over the summer. For all their effort, they had covered a little over three hundred miles of coast in a direct line. His lack of interest in rivers would return to haunt him later. They had found the mouths of the Skeena and the Nass, but Vancouver dismissed them as "too insignificant to be dignified by the name of rivers, and in truth scarcely deserve the appellation of rivulets." Certainly he was emphatic that neither "one of these brooks" was a navigable waterway. They had missed the mouth of the Stikine, but Vancouver was convinced that his survey of the coast so far would put an end to the theories of de Fuca, de Fonte "and other pretenders to a prior knowledge of these regions" that a strait connected the west coast with the interior of the continent. There was still the coast to the north, particularly Cook Inlet, to investigate. He pitted hope against experience, thinking that perhaps the worst was over and that next year's work "would be attended with less disappointment and fatigue." Right now, it was time to retire to a milder climate, "where refreshments might be obtained" and the crews could have some much deserved rest.[14] With all these matters in mind, Vancouver named the western entrance to Sumner Strait, the point where the second survey season ended, Cape Decision.

With the decision made, he wasted no time heading south. Whidbey's party returned to *Discovery* on Friday 20 September, and only contrary winds caused Vancouver to wait until Saturday to leave Port Protection. Vancouver chose to head

"View of Santa Barbara, on the Coast of California . . . ," monochrome watercolour by J. Sykes.

HYDROGRAPHIC OFFICE, TAUNTON, VIEW NO. 67

CAPE MENDOCINO *the South Promontory*

CAPE ORFORD

out to the open sea rather than follow the inside passages. Running down the west coast of the Queen Charlotte Islands, he had favourable though gentle winds and clear and pleasant weather. While they all enjoyed these few days of easy sailing, Vancouver was sufficiently attuned to the coast to suspect that it would not last: "The whales, seals, and sea otters, seemed to be aware of this, as great numbers of these animals had been sporting about us for the two or three previous days, enjoying the sunshine, and probably taking their leave of the summer season." By the time they reached the Scott Islands, the coast had changed its mood. In "adverse winds, calms, squally, thick, rainy, or foggy weather," it took more than a week to make the distance between the northern tip of Vancouver Island and Nootka Sound.[15]

He stayed only three days at Nootka. The new Spanish commander, Ramón Saavedra, had no new information, and *Daedalus*, which Vancouver was expecting, had not arrived. So there was no reason to tarry, and he sailed for the Spanish settlements to the south. He was disconcerted to find that the generous treatment of the previous year was not repeated either at San Francisco or Monterey. The changed Spanish attitude was a result of revised policy interpreted by different individuals. Vancouver missed Bodega, especially when he had to deal with Governor José Joaquín de Arrillaga, who was particularly frosty. Since the Spanish provided few supplies, Vancouver was relieved to meet up with *Daedalus* at sea between San Francisco and Monterey. The supply ship had returned to the coast from New South Wales with stores and provisions. Bodega's influence was behind the fact that Vancouver got a warmer welcome at San Diego, but there were no new instructions from London waiting there as he had hoped. He left San Diego to investigate the coast to the south and completed his survey to just below 30° north latitude on the coast of Baja California, "the southern limit of our intended survey of the western coast of North America."[16] With that, he turned away from the coast and set his course for Hawaii to the southwest.

On reaching the biggest of the Hawaiian Islands, he tried to anchor in Hilo Bay because it was Kamehameha's favourite residence. But the windward side of the island did not provide a satisfactory refuge, so the vessels sailed around to Kealakekua Bay. There they spent a very pleasant six weeks living on the beneficence of Kamehameha and his people, generously provided with hogs, fruit, vegetables and fresh water. Vancouver could not help but compare the openhandedness of "these untaught children of nature" with the miserable reception he had received from the "the educated civilized governor of New Albion and California." Vancouver also noted the harsh side of Hawaiian life, especially the absolute power of chiefs over their people. When a young commoner accidentally injured a chief's son while playing, his eyes were gouged out and he was left in that condition for two days before being executed by strangulation.[17] Yet Vancouver, like many Europeans, saw the Polynesians as the archetypal noble savages, and favourable comparisons between Hawaiian and European society occurred to Vancouver more than once during his last sojourn in the islands. "A conduct so disinterestedly noble, and uniformly observed by so untutored a race," as he described their hospitality, "will not fail to excite a certain degree of regret, that the first social principles, teaching mutual support and universal benevolence, should so frequently, amongst civilized people, be sacrificed to suspicion, jealousy and distrust."[18]

There were chores to take care of at Kealakekua Bay. An observatory was set up on shore. Repairs were made to the ships. The stores brought by *Daedalus* were transferred to *Discovery* and *Chatham*. *Daedalus* then left for New South Wales. Sailing in her on his way back to England was Thomas Pitt, a midshipman whom Vancouver had discharged for unsatisfactory behaviour. Though Pitt did not know it, in his absence from England he had become Baron Camelford on the death of his father, nor did Vancouver know that he had not seen the last of this troublesome crew member.

With the routine matters taken care of, he turned his attention to negotiations with Kamehameha and other chiefs on Hawaii. By his own account, Vancouver had developed a friendly relationship with the leaders at Kealakekua Bay. The memory of Cook still hung over the place, but Vancouver was prepared to forgive, if not forget, in the face of the hospitality he had received. He quickly decided, however, that it would not be possible to negotiate a peace between the leaders on Hawaii and those on the other islands. There was, he concluded, too much distrust between the various factions. Moreover, he was not prepared to put his ships through the wear and tear of running back and forth from one island to another in "boisterous weather" in an effort to bring peace. At this stage in the voyage, he needed to conserve his equipment and supplies.[19] It is also probable that Vancouver was, by now, too closely associated with Kamehameha to have much credibility with the chiefs on the other islands. Though he gave up the peace-making role, he still intended to persuade the Hawaiian leaders to cede their territory to Britain.

As a prelude to diplomacy, Vancouver established closer relations with Kamehameha through a little marriage counselling. He learned that the chief was estranged from his favourite wife, Kaahumanu. Kamehameha could not initiate a reconciliation without loss of face, so Vancouver took it upon himself to act as an intermediary. He contrived to have both aboard *Discovery* at the same time and

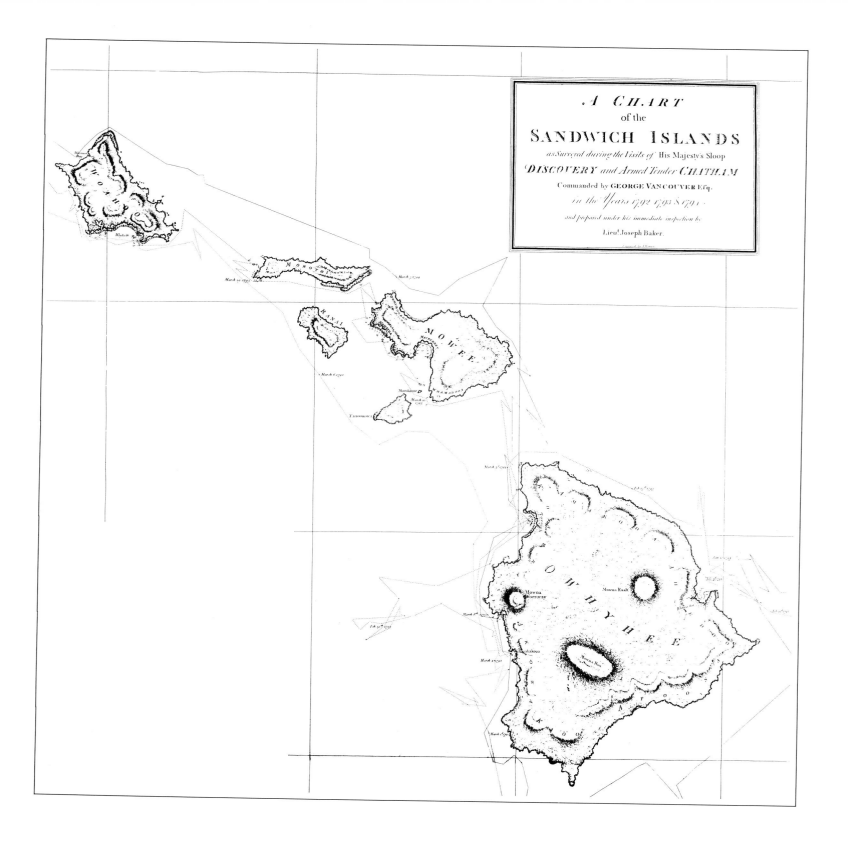

A CHART
of the
SANDWICH ISLANDS
as Surveyed during the Visits of His Majesty's Sloop
DISCOVERY and Armed Tender CHATHAM
Commanded by GEORGE VANCOUVER Esq.
in the Years 1792 1793 & 1794
and prepared under his immediate inspection by
Lieut. Joseph Baker.

positioned himself so that Kamehameha could not withdraw when Kaahumanu entered. Fortunately the stratagem worked, as the couple embraced with affection and pleasure at their reunion. It was a touching moment with which Vancouver was well pleased: "The domestic affairs of *Tamaahmaah* [Kamehameha] having thus taken so happy a turn, his mind was more at liberty for political considerations: and the cession of Owhyhee to His Britannic Majesty became now an object of his serious concern."[20]

Vancouver soon persuaded Kamehameha to cede Hawaii to Britain but then had to convince the sub-chiefs of the various districts. At a ceremony aboard *Discovery* on the morning of 25 February 1794, the leaders formally "ceded" Hawaii to Britain. Puget and a group of officers went ashore to plant the British flag, and salutes were fired from the vessels. The Hawaiian leaders certainly viewed the "cession" differently from Vancouver. Throughout the discussions they were clearly concerned with the advantages for them. Kamehameha and the other chiefs were mostly interested in getting British protection from the depredations of other Europeans and material assistance in their dynastic wars with leaders on the other islands. In the hope of further support, Hawaiian leaders continued to set some store by the British connection, even though the British government did not follow up on Vancouver's action.

With the "cession" complete, Vancouver got *Discovery* underway and sailed from Kealakekua Bay for the last time. He followed the western coastline of Hawaii, sailing on "a serene, tranquil ocean, fanned by a gentle breeze." The land to starboard "rose with a gradual ascent from the sea shore, seemed to be in a high state of cultivation, and was interspersed with a great number of extensive villages."[21] They enjoyed a few days of pleasant sailing which, within a month, far to the north, they would recall with some nostalgia. Travelling in *Discovery* along the Hawaiian coast, Kamehameha was generous to the end. He presented Vancouver with a gift of nearly one hundred hogs and a huge quantity of vegetables. After Vancouver said an emotional good-bye to the Hawaiian leader, a breeze from the land took the expedition away towards Maui.

Vancouver wanted to complete his survey of the Hawaiian Islands by mapping parts of the coast of Maui, Oahu and Kauai. That task was done by mid-March. The last island he visited was Niihau, the westernmost in the group. Vancouver then fixed the location of a small and isolated island that he called Bird Island, now known as Nihoa, and then "our course was directed to the northward."[22]

FACING PAGE: *Recollecting there was a large cove to the northward . . . I sat out after dinner to take a view of it, and finding it a very eligible place, I returned in the evening, and with the flood tide the following morning, we stood towards this bay . . . which I distinguished by the name of* RESTORATION COVE.

About the shores and on the rocks, we found some species of the . . . common gull.

In one of these [bays] they stopped at breakfast, where finding some muscles, a few of the people ate of them roasted; as had been their usual practice when any of these fish were met with.

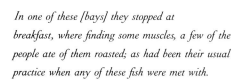

FACING PAGE: *The party . . . discovered an extensive deserted village, computed to have been the residence of nearly three hundred persons. It was built on a rock, whose perpendicular cliffs were nearly inaccessible on every side; and connected with the main, by a low narrow neck of land.*

In the morning of the 9th, they bent their way up this channel, . . . and found the shores composed of steep rocky cliffs, difficult to land upon, though but moderately elevated; their lower parts being well wooded, but towards their summits rugged and barren.

Having now completed the examination of this branch,
the party returned along its northern shores. . . . In their
way they saw several bears; two young cubs were killed,
and proved excellent eating.

Numberless whales enjoying the season, were playing
about the ship in every direction.

IV

THIRD SEASON

The Shape of Reality

VANCOUVER HAD DECIDED TO REVERSE HIS PATTERN of the last two summers and work instead from north to south. He therefore headed for Cook Inlet, or, as he still called it, Cook's River, at the northern end of the Northwest Coast. The plan was to carry the survey from there south towards Cape Decision where he had left off the previous fall. Having examined the coast between 30° and 56° north latitude without finding any major waterway through the continent, the next most likely entrance to the northwest passage in the minds of theoretical geographers was Cook's River. Investigating that part of the coast was now his most important task. Vancouver also felt that it would be the most laborious part of the work left to be done. Furthermore, this strategy had the advantage of starting the third survey season from a known point, for Vancouver had been there with Cook in 1778. But, that time, he had been there in May and June.

The drawback of Vancouver's approach in 1794 was that, heading towards the high latitudes in late March, his men had to contend with the bitter, biting cold. As he approached the northern land, the "climate began to assume a degree of severity that was new to us; . . . the mercury stood at the freezing point, and for the first time during the voyage the scuttle cask on the deck was frozen." He sighted land near Chirikof Island and followed the coast of Kodiak and Afognak Island to enter Cook Inlet on 12 April 1794. The weather was reasonably mild, and Vancouver was surprised to see flocks of wild geese flying southward. He should have taken more notice of this omen, for there was soon "a very material alteration" in the weather. The wind changed and brought frost and snow, the temperature dropped to 23° Fahrenheit at night, and, though the next morning dawned bright and clear, "the air was so excessively keen, that the sun's rays had no effect on the thermometer."[1] Farther up the inlet, Vancouver worried about the

FACING PAGE: *I directed our course towards the intricate inhospitable labyrinth, lying between us and the point I was so anxious to gain; in the hope, that amongst the numerous islets and rocks, some place of secure anchorage might be found.*

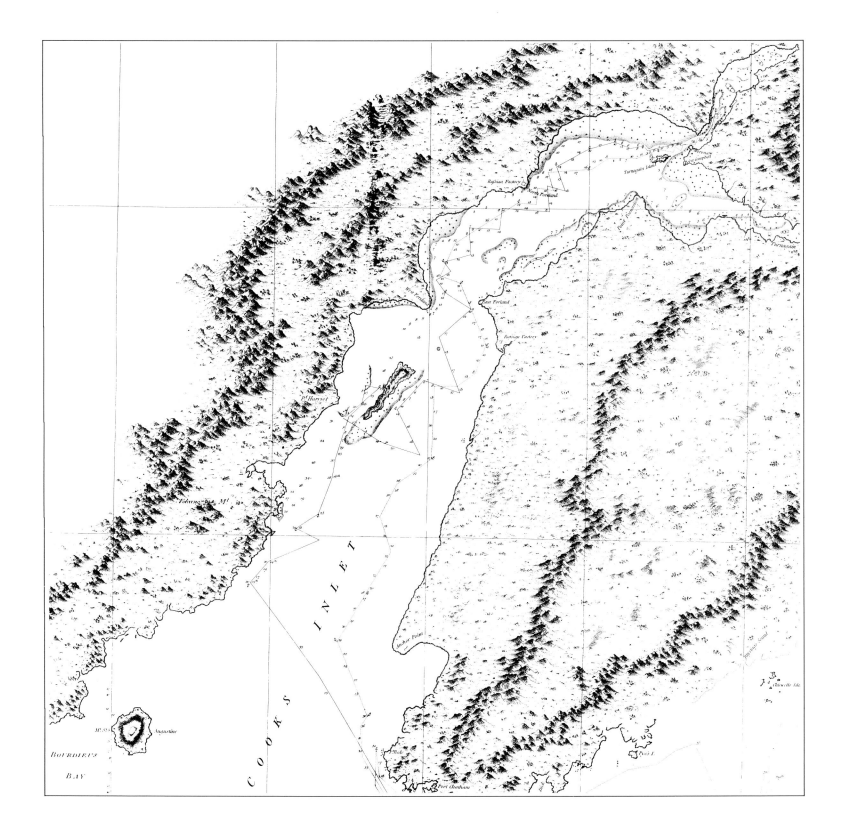

ice floes that were moving about in the area's particularly strong tides. When huge pieces of ice crashed against the bow of *Discovery*, he feared that the hull would sustain major damage. The boats were even more vulnerable, and Vancouver fretted more than usual about the safety of his crews, especially when they were behind schedule returning to the vessels. To add to the dangers, the inlet was full of rocks and shoals that were made particularly hazardous by the huge tides. In some parts of the inlet the daily range of the tide was more than thirty feet. *Discovery* went aground in several places, though each time she floated off without significant damage. The conditions were the worst that they had faced in three years on the coast, but the survey continued.

As he entered Cook Inlet, Vancouver was particularly conscious that he was sailing in the wake of the great navigator. Yet he perhaps also knew that Cook had been at the end of his tether in those northern waters. Worn out from the years of voyaging, Cook had lost his drive for discovery and had not pushed himself as hard as he once would have done.[2] He had gone up the inlet to the point where it splits into Turnagain and Knik arms and thought that he had found a major river. But, incredibly for Cook, he had considered it "nothing but a triffling point in Geography" and moved on.[3] Cook had not discovered the northwest passage, but he left an opening a mile wide for the theoretical geographers. Peter Pond was prompted to speculate that "Cook's River" flowed into Great Slave Lake, and the government of Great Britain rekindled its interest in the possibility of a northwest passage. It was up to Vancouver to determine the shape of reality.

He sailed up the inlet as far as Cook had gone. It was difficult to find a safe anchorage amongst the numerous shoals, but he finally found one near Fire Island. Then the boats were sent out. It took Whidbey two days to determine that Cook's Turnagain River was in fact an inlet. Vancouver himself, accompanied by Baker and Menzies, rowed up Knik Arm, and, in less than a day, found themselves within sight of the end of that inlet. Like so much of the coast, the whole area was surrounded by lofty mountains that "appeared to form an uninterrupted barrier." Vancouver therefore concluded that "according to the general acceptation of geographical terms, this can be no longer considered as a *river*; I shall therefore distinguish it henceforth as an *inlet*." He renamed the body of water Cook Inlet, though, in doing so, he was being somewhat critical of his mentor. For, had Cook "dedicated one day more to its further examination, he would have spared the theoretical navigators, who have followed him in their closets, the task of ingeniously ascribing to this arm of the ocean a channel, through which a north-west passage existing according to their doctrines, might ultimately be discovered."[4] Implicitly, he was also suggesting that Cook might have saved both

"Port Dick," monochrome watercolour by H. Humphrys. HYDROGRAPHIC OFFICE, TAUNTON, VIEW NO. 34

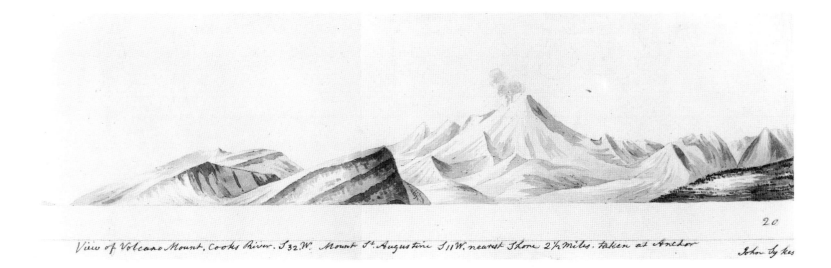

View of Volcano Mount, Cooks River. J 32.W. Mount J.t. Augustine J.11.W. nearest Shore 2½ Miles. taken at Anchor

20

John Sykes

"View of Volcano Mount, Cooks River...,"
watercolour over pencil by J. Sykes. BANCROFT
LIBRARY, BERKELEY, ROBERT B. HONEYMAN
COLLECTION, NO. 598

Vancouver and his men from a good deal of hardship and discomfort.

Having established the coastline of Cook Inlet, the expedition moved over to the next major indentation in the Alaskan coast: Prince William Sound. The survey was completed by two boat expeditions, one led by Whidbey and the other by Johnstone. Whidbey was given the task of following the coastline from Cape Puget at the western entrance of the sound right around to Snug Corner Cove, Cook's anchorage near the entrance of Port Fidalgo on the eastern side of the sound. It was a tough, gruelling expedition that took nearly three weeks and covered something like 420 miles.[5] They were often delayed by violent weather, and on one occasion a huge avalanche ripped down the mountainside not a hundred yards from where they were camped. As they rowed to the heads of the inlets, they were confronted with towering walls of ice where glaciers met the sea. At first, they were unable to explain the great rumbling noises, "not unlike loud, but distant thunder," that reverberated around them.[6] They soon realized that they were hearing the sound of huge pieces of ice breaking off the faces of glaciers to crash into the sea. In spite of these hazards, Whidbey completed a careful survey of the perimeter of the sound around to the point where Johnstone was to take over.

Meanwhile, Vancouver instructed Johnstone to follow the east coast of Prince William Sound, from Snug Corner Cove to its entrance, and then down the open coast to Cape Suckling. Like Vancouver, Johnstone had been in the sound before: in his case, with James Colnett in the *Prince of Wales* in 1788. But he now mapped the western shore more accurately than any one else had done. Within the sound,

"Port Dick, near Cook's Inlet," sketch by H.
Humphrys, engraved by B. T. Pouncy. VANCOUVER,
A VOYAGE, VOL. III, P. 151

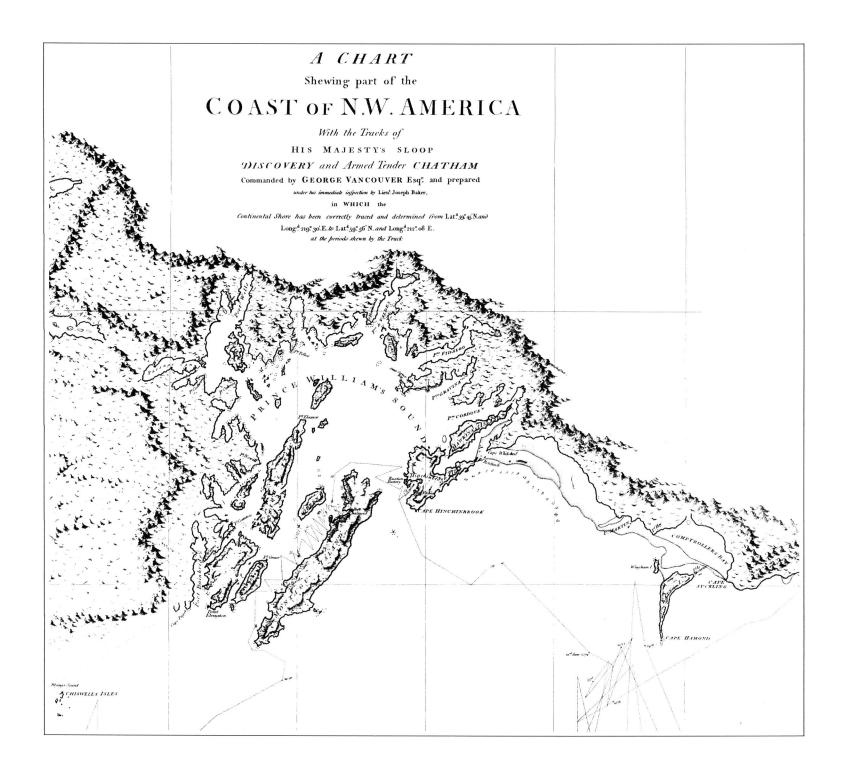

he faced the same weather as Whidbey. On the same day that the other party narrowly escaped the avalanche, Johnstone sat out a storm that blew with greater fury than any he had ever experienced in all his years at sea. When he reached the opening to the ocean between Point Whitshed and Hinchinbrook Island, the surf was so tremendous that it was impossible to get the boats through. The crew had run out of supplies and Johnstone did not want to risk their lives along the open coast. And yet it was still with some reluctance that he returned to *Discovery* before he had completed his allotted task. The survey of the inside of Prince William Sound was complete, though they were already into the second half of June.

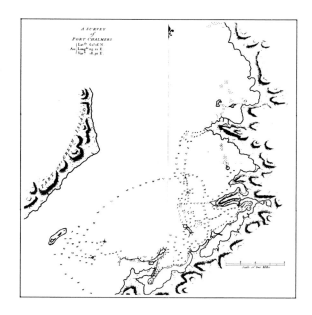

In Cook Inlet and, to a lesser extent, Prince William Sound, the expedition made contact with a number of native groups. They seemed to be mild-mannered people who showed no hostility towards Vancouver's men. On one occasion Johnstone was a bit uneasy when he camped for the night near a large group of native people, but there were no violent incidents. Vancouver had some inkling of the cultural diversity of the area, but it is difficult to tell which specific group he met at each encounter. The area was a meeting place of cultures. There were Chugach Eskimo groups, as Prince William Sound was the easternmost region inhabited by Eskimo on the south coast of Alaska. The Tanaina, an Athapaskan group, had moved into the area prior to European contact and adopted some aspects of Chugach culture. Tlingit Indians from the south sometimes traded this far north, and the cultural pattern was made even more complex by the fact that Russian fur traders imported Aleuts as labourers.[7]

The Russian influence on all of these people was clear from the beginning. The first group to come aboard *Discovery* showed that they were acquainted with European manners by "bowing very respectfully on coming upon deck." Vancouver was also fairly sure that many of them knew a number of Russian words, though he could not be certain since he knew neither the indigenous language nor Russian. He later realized that many of these native people were very much under the thumbs of "their Russian masters."[8]

The Russians had recently established permanent fur-trading posts on the coast. The *promyshlenniki* (fur traders) had initially come to the islands and coast of the Gulf of Alaska only as temporary residents for the fur-hunting season. Then during the 1780s, between Vancouver's first and second visit to the area, permanent fur-trading posts had been established in both Cook Inlet and Prince William Sound. The Russians had not yet established posts any farther along the coast than Prince William Sound, but they were making trading excursions eastward to Cape Suckling and beyond. They were finding, as would Vancouver, that the northern Tlingit were a good deal more aggressive than the native people of Cook Inlet and Prince William Sound. Already there had been at least one serious dispute with the people of Yakutat Bay. The Russian fur trade in the north developed along different lines from the maritime fur trade on the southern coast. Rather than trading through middlemen, the Russians coerced the native hunters into working directly for them. These hunters were forced to give up their furs, and the Aleuts in particular became virtual serfs. Initially, the Russians were able to impose this system of compulsory labour, and Vancouver saw little sign of hostility, but eventually it would lead to conflict.

Members of the British expedition visited some of the Russian posts. The Russians were friendly enough, though they made it clear from the start that the area "belonged exclusively to the Russian empire."[9] The British, however, were wholly unimpressed with these outposts of empire, commenting mostly on the filth and stink around the settlements. Apparently the fur traders were in the habit of throwing out their household garbage around the perimeter of their dwellings during winter, and now, with spring thaw, it produced "a most intolerable stench." Vancouver was also critical of the fact that they had made no effort to cultivate the soil, which he presumed to be capable of producing food in summer. He commented revealingly that "they appeared to be perfectly content to live after the manner of the native Indians of the country." In fact, he went on, it was difficult to see much difference between the two groups. Vancouver's men did not tarry at any of these Russian settlements. They paid one last visit to a post in Port Etches at the entrance to Prince William Sound, but, according to Vancouver, it "afforded little worthy of attention besides what has already been described."[10] With that parting comment, he proceeded down the coast.

Puget was sent ahead in *Chatham* to examine the coastline to the southeast of Prince William Sound. The two vessels would meet up in Yakutat Bay or, failing that, Cross Sound. Vancouver hoped for clear and easy sailing down the coast, but his passage proved to be stormy and difficult. It took nearly two weeks to reach Yakutat Bay. He used the time to record some reflections in his journal, adding general observations of the area that he had just surveyed and wondering, once again, why Cook had been so casual about detail when he was there. This apparent inattention to nautical matters was so uncharacteristic "of that justly renowned and most celebrated navigator" that Vancouver incorrectly attributed blame to the editor of Cook's *A Voyage to the Pacific Ocean*.[11] Yet, he too was discovering the difficulties of hydrography in northern waters. The bad weather and contrary winds prevented him from entering Yakutat Bay and joining the *Chatham*. Fortunately Puget had surveyed both the bay and the adjacent coast. The skies cleared enough to see the two mountains, Mount St. Elias and Mount

FACING PAGE: *To have landed amongst these people, who appeared to be so watchful and to keep themselves so readily on their defence, could have answered no good purpose; nor would it have been prudent, for the sake of a more minute, though perhaps not less equivocal, inquiry into these mysterious ceremonies, to have attempted a further acquaintance, at the risk of any misunderstanding. For these reasons, therefore, they were left in quiet possession of their dreary rocks; every inch of which they seemed disposed to have disputed.*

"A View from the Anchorage in Port Etches: Prince Williams Sound," monochrome watercolour by H. Humphrys. HYDROGRAPHIC OFFICE, TAUNTON, VIEW NO. 35

Fairweather, that dominate that part of the coast. He also noticed, but did not investigate, Lituya Bay.

On 7 July they were heading towards a prominent, high bluff that proved to be Cape Spencer, the northern entrance to Cross Sound. Vancouver felt his way into the sound and found an anchorage in Port Althorp at the northern end of Chichagof Island. *Chatham* joined *Discovery*, and repairs were made to the ships. Both had taken a pounding over the last three years, and replacement parts were running low. The sails and rigging on *Discovery* needed work that "called forth all our management and ingenuity" because they had so little good rope left.[12] It was fortunate, then, that they were about to commence the last leg of the coastal survey.

Nor was it just the vessels that were showing signs of wear and tear. Vancouver's health had been poor since the beginning of the voyage, and now there were times when he was completely incapacitated. So far, since arriving on the northern coast for the third season, his health had been so poor that, apart from brief outings like the one in Cook Inlet, he had not led any of the major boat excursions during the summer of 1794. He anticipated that the last stretch of coastline, from Cross Sound south, would be a complicated one, and so, while Whidbey examined the continental shore, he planned to survey the offshore islands. He set out early one morning with a boat crew, but by noon he had to return to *Discovery*, having been "seized with a most violent indisposition, which terminated in a bilious cholic." He was confined to his cabin for several days.[13] While Vancouver

FACING PAGE: *On the base of this singular rock, which, from its resemblence to the Light House rock off Plymouth, I called the* NEW EDDYSTONE, *we stopped to breakfast. . . . The fissures and small chasms in its sides, quite up to its summit, afforded nourishment to some small pine trees and various shrubs. The south and eastern part of its base is an intire bed of sand.*

"Mount Fairweather," monochrome watercolour by *H. Humphrys.* HYDROGRAPHIC OFFICE, TAUNTON, VIEW NO. 37

seldom gave much detail about his state of health, he was clearly very ill by the third season on the coast. He was increasingly prone to outbursts of temper, and, more to his credit, he constantly worried about the welfare of his crews.

If Vancouver was feeling the effects of four years of voyaging, then so too were his men. They had been through the same ordeals, and, compared to the officers, those below decks lived in harsher conditions and survived on an inferior diet. Vancouver insisted that their quarters be cleaned and aired regularly, and, as conditions allowed, he did his best to provide healthy food. The spruce beer, for example, proved to be particularly fine at Port Althorp. The hazards facing the boat parties were also very much on Vancouver's mind, perhaps all the more so since he could not take part. Even in late July the survey of the Cross Sound area was going to be "a very irksome and tedious task" because of the huge chunks of ice that were floating everywhere in the water. Instead of the usual two boats, he sent Whidbey off on an excursion with three as a little extra insurance against accidents.[14]

Whidbey was to examine Cross Sound, and, as it turned out, the many bays and inlets that branched off it. He was gone for more than two weeks. Beginning at Cape Spencer at the northern entrance to Cross Sound, he followed the coastline past Taylor and Dundas bays to the much larger Glacier Bay, which was sealed off by great walls of ice at the foot of the glaciers. Then he followed Icy Strait to the point where it met with Chatham Strait and Lynn Canal. He examined the canal first, up the west side and down the east. Coming out of Lynn Canal, he saw the northern end of Stephens Passage but thought that it was closed off and therefore a bay rather than an inlet that opened into Frederick Sound to the south. Thinking that Admiralty Island was a part of the mainland, he instead followed Chatham Strait, a wide, clear passage that stretched away to the south. When he reached the southern tip of Admiralty Island, he could see the open Pacific between Cape Ommaney and Cape Decision, the point where they had left off last summer. Again, Whidbey had navigated a maze of waterways under trying conditions, and now the end was in sight. But they had run out of supplies, were extremely cold and wet, and were more than one hundred miles away

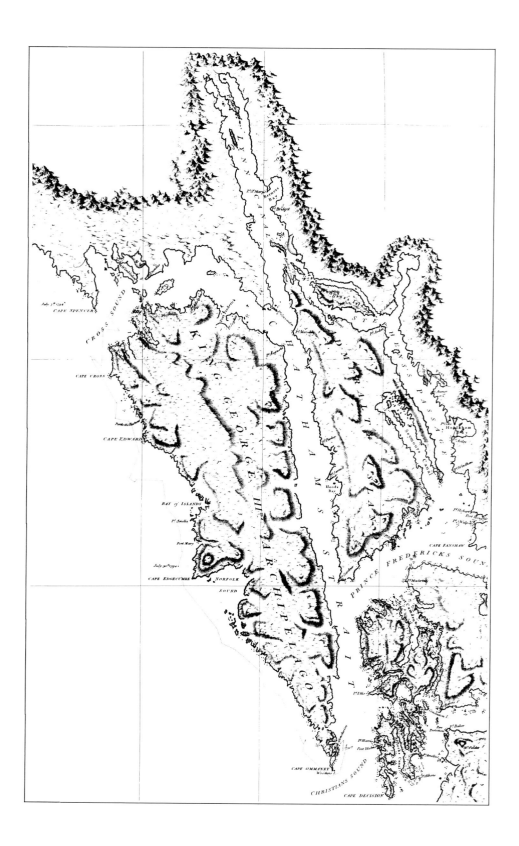

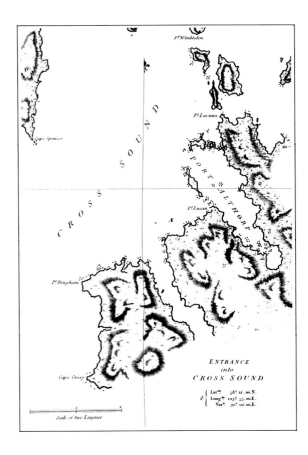

ENTRANCE
into
CROSS SOUND

Lat.º 58º 12'.00.N.
Long.º 223º 55'.00.E.
Var.º 30º 00'.00.E.

Scale of two Leagues

from the ships. Whidbey had no choice but to turn back and head for *Discovery*.

Once Whidbey had reported his findings, Vancouver decided to sail the vessels down the coast to find another anchorage. This move would enable him to delineate the open coastline and also save his boat crews from having to run the risk of travelling through the ice in Cross Sound again. Two days took them down to Cape Ommaney, and, entering Chatham Strait, they found a sheltered harbour a few miles up the east coast of Baranof Island. Here *Discovery* and *Chatham* were prepared for the long homeward journey, while the last boat parties were sent out to complete the coastal survey. As had so often been the case, they were led by Whidbey and Johnstone. Their final task was to examine the ramifications of Frederick Sound, with Whidbey following the north shore and Johnstone the south. Since the coastal space left to be examined occupied about one degree of latitude, Vancouver hoped that it would take about a week. By now, he should have known better. Floating ice had become less of a problem, but they faced a lot of wet, gloomy weather, and, as always, the boat crews found unexpected twists and turns around every corner of the coast. Yet, when the boats had not returned even after two weeks, Vancouver was not primarily concerned about the hazards of navigation, having every confidence in the ability of his officers and men to handle any crisis of weather or water. He was, however, very concerned about what appeared to be the growing hostility of the people of the coast.

Since arriving in Cross Sound, the expedition had been, once again, working in Tlingit territory. This northern group was particularly aggressive in its response to Europeans and challenged Whidbey's boat crews on several occasions. In Lynn Canal there was an incident that was very like the fatal confrontation the previous summer in Behm Canal. Whidbey's party was joined by a single canoe of Indians, led by a man whose dignified manner and fine dress left them in no doubt of his rank and authority. The initial contact was friendly enough, but as the boat crew pulled into a small cove for the night, Whidbey was on his guard. By morning, the number of Indians had swelled to one or two hundred, and they were making hostile moves towards the boats. As well as spears and daggers, some of the Tlingit had muskets and were perfectly familiar with their use. Whidbey's suspicions had prepared him for an attack, and he was able to get the boats off the shore and away, but it was a very touchy moment that could easily have resulted in disaster. Nor was it the last such incident. A couple of days later Whidbey was prevented from entering Stephens Passage by a threatening group of Tlingit. Then later, on his last boat trip, as he followed Stephens Passage from the south, he encountered the same group again. Taking no chances, Whidbey

"Icy Bay and Mount St. Elias," sketch by T. Heddington, engraved by J. Fittler. VANCOUVER, A *VOYAGE,* VOL. III, P. 204

had a warning shot fired at the canoes, and, when that failed to deter them, he fired into a canoe. The Indians then withdrew, and later that evening the seamen heard what they thought were the sounds of lamentation coming from the Tlingit village. With reports like these coming in from his boat crews, Vancouver was keenly aware of the growing atmosphere of tension with the native people on this part of the coast.

Under these circumstances, it was little wonder that he was troubled when the final boat expeditions were more than a week late returning. As he grew more anxious by the hour, Vancouver reflected on the likely causes of this hostility. He was inclined to blame the behaviour of Europeans rather than considering the possibility that the Indians may have had their own reasons for harassing the intruders. By this late stage Vancouver's men were impatient to move along and finish the survey, and they could not have had many trade items left. As smooth relations were not being fostered by the exchange of goods, the Tlingit tried to get what they could by plunder. Vancouver's explanation had more to do with his faith in the superiority of European technology, particularly when it came to weapons. He again berated those fur traders who had provided the coastal Indians with firearms. He argued that native people would not normally have had the courage to attack Europeans, but, now they had become familiar with guns, they were emboldened to do so. Somewhat contradictorily, Vancouver claimed that the Indians now knew the destructive power of firearms in their own hands and, at the same time, no longer feared them in the hands of white men. In fact, firearms do not seem to have been a critical factor on the Indian side of these violent encounters. Though some had guns, they seemed to prefer to get close enough to use traditional hand-to-hand weapons. Still, Vancouver was convinced that, given the growing antagonism of native people and its causes as he saw them, a survey such as his, conducted from small, vulnerable boats, would be impossible just one year later.[15]

Vancouver did his best to allay his fears for his men who were out in the boats by throwing himself into the preparations for departure. The ploy was not entirely successful, however, and he "remained in the most uncomfortable state of suspense that can be imagined until Tuesday the 19th [August 1794]; when, in the midst of a deluge of rain, with the wind blowing very strong from the S.E. we had the indescribable satisfaction of seeing the four boats enter the harbour together from the northward." Vancouver's men reported that they had completed the coastal survey. Or, as Vancouver, put it in his matter-of-fact prose, they "communicated the glad tidings of their having effectually performed the service, and attained the object that had been expected from this expedition."[16]

After they had taken some time to recover, Whidbey and Johnstone reported more fully on their final boat trips. Whidbey had traversed the west coast of Chatham Strait and the northern shore of Frederick Sound until he reached the southern entrance of Stephens Passage, which he had thought was a bay when he had earlier approached it from the north. This time he rowed the length of the passage and also examined its side issue, Taku Inlet, with its great glacier. He then followed Frederick Sound to the south as far as the mouth of the Stikine River where Johnstone had been the previous summer. Whidbey then turned and headed back up the sound. About halfway up the waterway, on a rare fine day, he landed on a beach so the men could eat, dry their clothes and clean out the boats, but they were obliged to make a hasty retreat by a threatening group of Indians. This time, Whidbey was very relieved to see Johnstone's boat party approaching. Johnstone had covered the east coast of Chatham Strait from Cape Decision around into Frederick Sound. From there, he took Keku Strait, running between Kupreanof and Kuiu islands, that he had missed a year ago. Returning to Frederick Sound, he followed it round to the meeting with Whidbey.

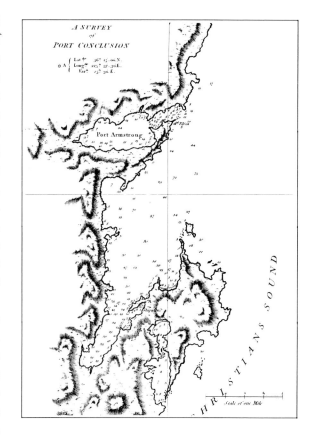

It was appropriate that the superb coastal survey should be completed by the coming together of the two boat crews in the remote reaches of Frederick Sound. Day after day, they had done the hard work along lonely reaches of coastline. As they had done so often before, they found a small cove and went ashore to dine and spend the night. There were congratulations all around, and a sailors' celebration was held in the absence of their austere commanding officer. Amidst the merriment, the seamen wondered if the whole expedition had not, after all, been just an April fools' joke. They had sailed from England on the first of April and spent four years searching for a nonexistent passage in the wake of de Fuca and de Fonte "and a numerous train of hypothetical navigators." The notion produced "no small portion of facetious mirth" amongst the seamen that evening. The following day there was a rather more formal ritual as Whidbey took "possession" of that part of the coast with as much ceremony as they could muster under the circumstances, "and a double allowance of grog was served to the respective crews, for the purpose of drinking His Majesty's health." Back at *Discovery* and *Chatham* there was another round of rather more restrained celebration. After more grog was served, mutual congratulations were passed between the vessels in the form of "three exulting cheers."[17] In honour of the occasion, Vancouver named his last anchorage Port Conclusion.

Though it does not show in his writing, Vancouver was both elated and relieved that the tremendous task was completed. As he often did when describing moments of high emotion, he left the appreciation of his men's feelings to the reader's imagination. He believed that such things were "more easily conceived than explained."[18] Only the members of the expedition could really know the satisfaction that came from the completion of the survey. Vancouver took great pride in his officers, but he also knew that the work could not have been done without the seamen who did the manual labour under trying conditions. He had pressed them hard, and they had responded. Largely under sheer manpower, the boats had travelled more than ten thousand miles during the three seasons of surveying.[19] As for himself, Vancouver was a little defensive that he had exceeded the letter of his instructions and pursued the survey with such vigour for so long. Yet now he had brought it to a successful conclusion. He had traced the Pacific coastline of North America from top to bottom and, as far as he was concerned, absolutely disproved the existence of anything resembling a northwest passage. Nor were the discoveries that resulted from his exploration merely negative ones.

He had learned much about the coastline that could not have been foretold. At times he paid tribute to those who, earlier in his career, had taught him the navigational skills by which to "traverse and delineate these lonely regions."[20] He had come to the coast to impose the straight lines of latitude and longitude, as if the shoreline could be boxed in by science and a lineage of logic. After three seasons of surveying, he knew better. He had, he later reported, examined the coast, from Baja California in the south to Cook Inlet in the north, "through all of the various turnings and windings."[21] During the process, the coast had not easily surrendered its secrets. It was always a force with which to reckon. And Vancouver had learned that the people of the coast could not be ignored. They too were a determining factor in any coastal enterprise. While their co-operation had facilitated the survey in the south, the hostility of the Tsimshian and Tlingit had threatened the successful completion of the task in the north.

With the work done, Vancouver was anxious to be sailing homeward. He was ready to leave when the boat crews returned, but the coast continued to have its say. A violent gale blew from the southeast, his intended direction, and with it came heavy rain and fog. The wind raged for four days before it abated somewhat and he decided to put to sea. Still the coast did not give up easily. It took two days to make the few miles out to the open ocean, and, in the process, the vessels were nearly wrecked on the rocks around Cape Ommaney. At the last minute they were saved by a gentle breeze from the northwest that blew them offshore, though not before a seaman was lost overboard. Vancouver finished his work on the coast as it had begun, in the teeth of a gale.

He sailed south to Nootka Sound for a final visit and one last effort to settle the outstanding issues with the Spanish. He arrived at Nootka at the beginning of

FACING PAGE: *The depth of water along the edge of the shoal was from two immediately to ten fathoms at high water; many unsuccessful attempts were made at this time to pass it, but the depth decreased too fast to venture further, and as the tide fell, patches of dry sand became visible in all directions.*

They met such innumerable huge bodies of ice, . . . as rendered their further progress up the branch rash, and highly dangerous. This was, however, very fortunately, an object of no moment, since before their return they had obtained a distinct view of its termination about two leagues further in the same direction, by a firm and compact body of ice reaching from side to side, and greatly above the level of the sea.

FACING PAGE: They frequently heard a very loud rumbling noise, not unlike loud, but distant thunder. . . . They now found the noise to originate from immense ponderous fragments of ice, breaking off from the higher parts of the main body, and falling from a very considerable height.

September to find a new Spanish commissioner, José Manuel de Alava, but no new instructions from either the British or the Spanish government. There was news that Vancouver would have preferred not to hear. He was saddened to learn of the death of Bodega earlier in the year. Dealings with the Spanish had never been as pleasant as they were when Bodega was their representative. His successor, Alava, still hoped that dispatches were on the way, so Vancouver agreed to wait at Nootka until the middle of October. Having surveyed the coast, he wanted to conclude the second part of his commission and settle the disagreement over Nootka Sound. There also was work to be done on the ships before they sailed, and on-shore observations to be taken. But for sailors eager to be on their way, the delay was frustrating.

With some time on his hands, Vancouver decided to pay another visit to Maquinna at Tahsis. Maquinna and some other chiefs had already been aboard *Discovery*, and this time had "received such compliments as were suitable to their rank." Now Vancouver would reciprocate. Alava and a party of Spanish officers accompanied a number of his own gentlemen on the excursion up Nootka Sound. Vancouver still worried about security, insisting that the boats carry the usual armaments even though he believed that the people of Nootka were friendly. At sunset they approached the head of Tahsis Inlet and camped overnight on an open piece of land in order to make a ceremonial entry into the village the following morning. They were given an effusive welcome and led to Maquinna's house where they were seated according to their rank. Vancouver was a less critical and more perceptive observer of the proceedings this time. Maquinna made a speech in which he apparently said that he was honoured by the visit, which he saw as an outcome of the peaceful relations that his people had maintained with the Europeans. He drew a contrast with other groups on the west coast of Vancouver Island, like Wickaninnish's people, who had attacked European vessels. As a consequence of his policy, he continued, Nootka Sound had been visited more frequently by traders and the wealth of his people had risen above that of any of their neighbours. Vancouver seemed to understand something of the Indian leader's need to maintain his position in relation to other groups and the extent to which he was using his visitor to achieve that end. When Maquinna danced wearing a mask, Vancouver still found the music "as offensive to the ear" as the dancing was "to the eye," but this time he tried to enter into the spirit of the occasion, recognizing the skill with which Maquinna changed masks and the enthusiasm of the performance. After a mutual exchange of presents, the visitors walked about the village. Vancouver recorded some details about the appearance of things. He was particularly impressed by the immense beams that formed the frames of the

"View of the land over the Bay of Bueno Esperanza . . . ," monochrome watercolour by J. Sykes. HYDROGRAPHIC OFFICE, TAUNTON, VIEW NO. 47

FACING PAGE: *To the north and east of this point, the shores of the continent form two large open bays, which were terminated by compact solid mountains . . . rising perpendicularly from the water's edge.*

houses and noted that Maquinna's was the largest of the habitations at Tahsis. He later saw what he took to be further evidence of Maquinna's power and authority when he visited the village of a lesser chief in Tlupana Inlet. To his eyes, at least, the village was smaller and the people less orderly than at Tahsis.[22]

While there was diplomatic activity at Tahsis with Maquinna, there was none at Friendly Cove with Alava. As the mid-October deadline approached and no new information arrived from Europe, Vancouver became more and more exasperated. He wrote to a friend in early October that he was "once more entrap'd in this infernal Ocean" without being sure when he would get out.[23] When 15 October arrived and there was still no news, he could wait no longer. He arranged to meet Alava in Monterey and put out to sea.

He had left it late in the season to sail southward. At first it did not seem to matter as a "light breeze from the land favored our progress out of Nootka," but just out of the sound he was caught in a fog bank and dead calm for two days.[24] Farther south he experienced the coast's other extreme in a storm that, excepting those off New Zealand at the other end of the Pacific, was the most violent he had sailed through. It ripped the foresail to shreds as he hauled off from the land. Unable to scud before the wind, he had to lie to and ride it out. The storm finally blew itself out, and, under an easy wind, he steered for Monterey.

He was made more welcome at the Spanish port than last year. The unfriendly Arrillaga had been replaced, and, once again, the expedition was provided with refreshments. There were no instructions from London, however. Vancouver decided that the British government would not expect him to stay on the coast any longer now that the survey was complete. Really, he had no choice but to leave. The men were worn out and so were the vessels. Vancouver was particularly concerned that *Discovery*, which had been aground several times, might have damage to her hull that he did not know about. One, at least, "of the great objects of our voyage, the survey of the coast of North West America, being now accomplished, . . . I did not long hesitate, but determined on making the best of my way towards England, by way of Cape Horn."[25]

Vancouver therefore left the coast with the Nootka Sound controversy unresolved. He did learn from Alava at Monterey that a new British commissioner had been appointed, but the Spaniard did not reveal that the appointment was intended for Vancouver. A revised Nootka Sound Convention had established that neither Britain nor Spain would have a permanent base at Nootka, though the ships of both nations would have access to the coast and both governments would prevent any third nation from asserting claims to the area. Spain had extracted herself from the conflict with good grace while Britain had made it clear that the

*"A Remarkable Mountain near the River of
Monterrey," sketch by J. Sykes, engraved by B. T.
Pouncy.* VANCOUVER, *A VOYAGE,* VOL. III, P. 334

Pacific was no longer a Spanish lake. "His Britannic Majesty" would not tolerate Spanish-imposed limitations on trade or empire on the Northwest Coast. In a ceremony in March 1795 at Nootka, the Spanish handed over the site of Meares's house to a British representative, and the Union Jack was run up a flagpole. A gesture that was rather more significant followed as the flag was handed over to Maquinna for safekeeping. The Indian leader must have been somewhat mystified by these empty rituals taking place on his land. Once the Spanish had gone, the native people dismantled the European buildings and rebuilt their own village. The question of sovereignty was settled, at least for the time being, as Friendly Cove became Yuquot once more.

The coast was still the domain of its native people. Though their lives were changing, they were not out of control, and the people remained independent and buoyant. Vancouver was on the coast during the peak years of the maritime fur trade, a trade in which the native poeple were equal partners. Some groups would rise and fall in wealth and power as fur traders came to their villages and later, when the number of furs diminished, passed them by. The people of Nootka Sound faced declining expectations after 1800 that would again put a strain on Maquinna's leadership. The fur trade brought moments of violence and new diseases, but it also injected new wealth into the native cultures, contributing to an elaboration of ritual and art. The cultural balance sheet, like the trade itself, was evenly weighted during the early years of contact. Later in the history of the coast, the European presence would affect the native cultures profoundly, but not in the immediate wake of Vancouver.

Meanwhile, the voyager made his way back homeward. He sailed from Monterey at the beginning of December 1794, and it would be ten months before he sighted the British coast. The expedition stopped at Cocos Island, the Galapagos, and then at Valparaiso for repairs and supplies. Vancouver's instructions suggested that he might make a survey of the southern coast of South America, but he decided that it was out of the question. They rounded Cape Horn in the kind of weather for which it was infamous among sailors then headed up the Atlantic to St. Helena. Since Britain was at war with France, sailing north alone would be risky. While repairs were made to *Discovery*, Vancouver sent *Chatham* to Brazil where he hoped that it could join a convoy and return to England. Thus *Chatham* separated from *Discovery* and made her own way home. When she was ready to sail, *Discovery* left St. Helena and joined a convoy of prize vessels under naval escort. Sailing to the westward to avoid the French navy, they sighted land off the west coast of Ireland, and Vancouver anchored *Discovery* in the Shannon on 13 September 1795. The sailor was home from the sea.

"The Town of Valparaiso on the coast of Chili," sketch by J. Sykes, engraved by J. Heath. VANCOUVER, A *VOYAGE,* VOL. III, P. 403

A

VOYAGE OF DISCOVERY

TO THE

NORTH PACIFIC OCEAN,

AND

ROUND THE WORLD;

IN WHICH THE COAST OF NORTH-WEST AMERICA HAS BEEN CAREFULLY EXAMINED AND ACCURATELY SURVEYED.

Undertaken by HIS MAJESTY's Command,

PRINCIPALLY WITH A VIEW TO ASCERTAIN THE EXISTENCE OF ANY NAVIGABLE COMMUNICATION BETWEEN THE

North Pacific and North Atlantic Oceans;

AND PERFORMED IN THE YEARS

1790, 1791, 1792, 1793, 1794, and 1795,

IN THE

DISCOVERY SLOOP OF WAR, AND ARMED TENDER CHATHAM,

UNDER THE COMMAND OF

CAPTAIN GEORGE VANCOUVER.

IN THREE VOLUMES.

VOL. I.

LONDON:
PRINTED FOR G. G. AND J. ROBINSON, PATERNOSTER-ROW;
AND J. EDWARDS, PALL-MALL.

1798.

Reproduction of the title page from volume one of the first edition of George Vancouver's A Voyage of Discovery to the North Pacific Ocean and Round the World . . . , *published in 1798.*

The End of Dreaming

VANCOUVER LEFT *DISCOVERY* RIGHT AWAY to report to the Admiralty in London. Parting with the officers and men with whom he had shared so many joys and tribulations over such a long period was a sad moment. It had been almost four and a half years since they sailed from Falmouth. During that time they had lived and worked at close quarters on board, and routinely risked their lives in small boats to chart a distant coastline. Vancouver wrote, characteristically, that the emotion of their farewells was "more easily to be imagined than I have the power to describe."[1]

Vancouver has been criticized for his harsh and unbending treatment of his men, and there were times when the criticism was deserved. He had maintained his demeanour as the stern commander, holding the expedition together by rigid discipline almost to the end of the voyage. But on the final run between St. Helena and England, there was a moment that revealed more of the man. After a storm, *Discovery*'s pinnace was sent to check on one of the prize vessels, and then, as it was being hoisted back on board, there was an accident that smashed it to pieces. The boat was the one that Vancouver had used, and it had always brought him safely back to *Discovery*, whatever the danger. To see it destroyed before his eyes produced "an involuntary emotion." Yet he "was compelled to turn away to hide a weakness…I should have thought improper to have publicly manifested."[2] And now, taking his final leave, there could be little doubt of his commitment to the welfare of his crew, as he expressed his pride that he had brought nearly all of them safely back to England.

Vancouver had certainly taken good care of the physical health of his crew. Only six men out of a complement of something like two hundred had died during the voyage, and, for the times, that was an extraordinary achievement. Conditions were so bad on British naval vessels that during the ensuing wars with France, more seamen would die from disease than would be killed by the enemy.[3] Under Vancouver, scurvy, the seaman's scourge, was kept at bay by the frequent brewing of spruce beer and Menzies's prescription of the rob of lemon to those with early symptoms. Three crew members were lost in accidental drownings. Two died of illness, one from an infection caught at the Cape of Good Hope and another after eating mussels on the Northwest Coast, an early victim of red tide. Such physical ailments can be diagnosed from the accounts in the journals. The mental health of the crews is much more difficult to determine, but the death of one man who, apparently in a state of depression, took his own life, perhaps provides a clue. Certainly the psychological effects of long voyaging in cramped quarters, and often under brutal working conditions, must have been considerable, particularly on sailors who were not aboard by choice.

Leaving his crew to sail *Discovery* around to the Thames under escort, Vancouver hurried to the Admiralty where, as he prosaically put it, "I deposited my several documents."[4] Among these was a set of superb charts of the western coastline of North America. There was more than a little irony in the fact that Vancouver's maps were laid before Alexander Dalrymple, who had only just been appointed head of the Admiralty's Department of Hydrography. Dalrymple was one of those "theoretical navigators" whom Vancouver so despised, a strong believer in the chimerical southern continent and a powerful advocate of the notion of a northwest passage.[5] Cook had disabused him of the first idea, and now Vancouver presented the facts of the matter regarding the second. Having submitted his charts and provided an account of his expedition to the Admiralty, his next major task was to produce a published version of his voyage to the coast. To this work he devoted the rest of his life.

Unfortunately his time was short, for Vancouver returned from his voyage broken in health. He had, perhaps, taken better care of his men than he had of himself. Though he did not provide much detail, he had been ill throughout much of the voyage, suffering at times from weakness, pains in his muscles and joints, lack of appetite, and occasional bouts of nausea and vomiting. An exact diagnosis of Vancouver's illness is difficult. Some have concluded that he suffered from a thyroid deficiency while others believe that it was Bright's disease.[6] What is clear is that his health was bad at the start of the voyage and got worse throughout. He was very weak by the end of the third season on the coast, and he admitted to being "in a very feeble and debilitated state" at Cocos Island on the journey home.[7] On his return to England, he went to the Bristol Hot Springs for treatment, and then he settled in the quiet village of Petersham near Richmond to live out his

FACING PAGE: *The upper part of this arm, which after the place of my nativity, the town of Lynn in Norfolk, obtained the name of* LYNN CHANNEL, *approaches nearer to those interior waters of the continent, which are said to be known to the traders and travellers from the opposite side of America, than we had found the waters of the North Pacific penetrate in any former instance.*

days. Unlike Cook who died in a flurry of excitement on a Pacific shore, Vancouver returned to England, and, like an old soldier, seemed to fade away. Yet Vancouver's voyage killed him as surely as Cook's had. He lived for less than three years after coming home from the coast.

Vancouver's return was also marred by a debilitating and demeaning row with his former midshipman, Thomas Pitt, now Lord Camelford. Prior to his discharge in Hawaii, Camelford had been flogged two or three times on Vancouver's orders and on another occasion he had been put in irons for several days. Soon after Vancouver moved to Petersham, Camelford returned to England determined to have revenge. He was violent and irrational and immediately challenged his former captain to a duel. Vancouver refused to give him that satisfaction, but Camelford continued to make threats. A chance encounter on a London street led to an attack on Vancouver and his brother by Camelford which gained considerable notoriety in the city. Vancouver appealed to the Lord Chancellor, who managed to calm Camelford down, but it was only the young lord's departure for the West Indies that provided Vancouver with real security from physical attack. Personal attacks continued from other quarters, however, and Vancouver's reputation was sullied by assaults from his often powerful critics.

His final years ashore were not pleasant ones, and there may have been moments when Vancouver wished again for the relatively straightforward task of navigating the coast. He had been back in England for two years before the Admiralty made an offer of payment for the nearly five years that he had served as commander of the expedition. The sum of just over seven hundred pounds that Vancouver finally received after some negotiating was anything but generous. Vancouver continued to suffer from the disapprobation of the powerful Joseph Banks, who had never liked him. Banks had supported Menzies in his decision not to hand his journals over to Vancouver at the end of the voyage. Banks even argued at one point that Menzies had been "wholly under my orders," and he was pushing Menzies to scoop Vancouver by publishing his journal of the voyage first.[8] Vancouver, not unnaturally, took the view that since he was the commanding officer of the expedition, he should get the credit for its achievements.

While making his way through these reefs and shoals, Vancouver was preoccupied with what turned out to be a race with death to complete the manuscript of his voyage for publication. It is not hard to imagine an ailing sailor taking refuge from the contrary winds of personality and politics in preparing the record of his achievement for posterity. Unlike many other accounts of exploration of the time, such as those by Cook, Meares or Alexander Mackenzie, Vancouver's was not rewritten and embellished by a ghost writer or "editor." He was assisted by his

FACING PAGE: *We had now no reason for remaining in this port, which, in consequence of this visit, obtained the name* PORT CONCLUSION.

brother, John Vancouver, and he commissioned some of the best engravers to prepare the illustrations and charts. But Vancouver's *Voyage* was to be his own, reflecting his personality.

Like his survey of the coast, his published account would be meticulous and detailed. Though he respected the editor of Cook's third voyage, he was convinced that if Cook had lived and "superintended the publication of his own labours," errors would have been avoided. In Port Conclusion, when the survey of the coast was complete, Vancouver had written of the need to provide a very detailed account of his work in order to prevent further speculation by theoretical geographers. He therefore wanted his account of the coast to be "*as conclusive as possible.*" Yet he was also aware that it might be dull, realizing that describing the day-by-day work of the survey "will afford but little entertainment." He therefore warned the reader in the introduction that the purpose of his voyage was to obtain useful knowledge, and, in that spirit, he felt it was his duty to provide detailed information "in a way calculated to *instruct*, even though it should fail to *entertain.*"[9]

And so, through his last months, Vancouver laboured at his life's work. Preparation of the manuscript was constantly delayed by his declining health, and it was not quite finished when he died on 12 May 1798. The charts were completed, but the narrative of the voyage was not, having been taken up to Vancouver's arrival in Valparaiso in March 1795. The text of the remaining one hundred or so pages was completed by John Vancouver, who had worked on the project all along. George Vancouver's *A Voyage of Discovery to the North Pacific Ocean and Round the World; in which the Coast of North-West America has been Carefully Examined and Accurately Surveyed* appeared three or four months after his death, and, with its posthumous publication, the assessment of his contribution to knowledge began.

Vancouver's was the last, though certainly not the least, of the great Pacific voyages. When it was over, the task of opening up the Pacific to European view was complete, and few mysteries remained. In the words of one scholar, his voyage marked "the end of dreaming" about the North Pacific.[10] Vancouver's dogged persistence had replaced theoretical speculation with real, practical detail. Whereas Cook had portrayed the coast between Nootka Sound and Cook Inlet as a straight line, Vancouver had examined all its convolutions. He had charted an accurate delineation of the coastline and thereby revealed what did exist as well as what did not. He had eliminated the possibility of a navigable northwest passage through North America to connect Europe with the Orient. He was careful to leave no gap in his chart that could be seized upon by armchair geographers as the entrance to some imagined channel through the continent. Inevitably he had missed things, and his critics would still quibble, seizing, for example, on his neglect of rivers as a failing. Vancouver had left the Fraser, Skeena, Nass and Stikine rivers uncharted beyond their entrances because he did not believe that they were navigable passages. He had established, however, such major points of geography as the insularity of Vancouver Island, and, most importantly, he had examined, carefully and painstakingly, every foot of the continental shoreline.

He had also littered the coast with place names, nearly four hundred in all.[11] In his choice of names, Vancouver put his cultural stamp on the coast. And, because of the imperialism of the printed word and the power of the British Empire, a large proportion of them have survived. Most were English names, though there were some exceptions such as Behm Canal, named after the governor of Kamchatka who had been so hospitable to Cook's crewmen in 1779. Naval men (Chatham Strait, Cape Spencer, Gardner Canal) had their names affixed to the coast, along with politicians and prominent families (Grenville Channel, Pitt Island, Port Townshend). Crew members down to the rank of midshipman were honoured by Manby Point, Cape Mudge, Point Pigot, but not usually able seamen unless, like John Carter, they had come to an unhappy end. Some places, Point Wales for instance, were named after friends. There was also a Point Menzies, but Vancouver named nothing after Banks. Familiar places in England were recalled by Wimbledon Point and Port Snettisham. Other names, such as Anvil Island, described the shape of the land as he saw it, or, as in the case of Barren Islands, his impression of it. Another set of names recorded events during the survey: Cape Caution, Deception Pass, Escape Point, Foulweather Bluff, Protection Island, Safety Cove, Seduction Point. Not all his names have endured. The largest island off the coast is now called Vancouver Island, rather than Vancouver and Quadra Island as he would have had it. Bodega y Quadra's name has survived, attached to a much smaller island, and that is not unreasonable given their relative importance to the history of the coast.

With the publication of his *Voyage*, Vancouver's coastline was committed to paper and made permanent for others to see. Where his words failed or were insufficient, he referred the reader to his charts.[12] Once Vancouver had put the coast on the map, it could be copied, circulated and consulted by those who planned to follow where he had been. There was no northwest passage lancing through the continent towards Cathay, and so Atlantic sailors would have to come to the coast by more arduous routes. Yet, as ships' captains approached from the Pacific and needed to get their bearings, Vancouver's coast could be laid out on the chart table and a clear line would become visible through the haze of uncertainty.

George Vancouver opened up the coast to the world of enterprise and exploitation. By the turn of the nineteenth century the peak years of the maritime fur trade had passed, but other entrepreneurs would follow. In the 1820s the Hudson's Bay Company built forts and ran ships along the coast in an effort to gather its resources with greater efficiency. The fur traders were followed by settlers, miners, loggers and fishermen, who came to possess and exploit the sea and the land. One hundred years after his voyage, the littoral became Vancouver's coastline in another sense as a city that bears his name grew to be the metropolitan centre for the development of the British Columbia coast.

The native people of the coast had, in the long run, little reason to celebrate Vancouver's coming. He was not a particularly perceptive observer of the coastal populations, yet he understood that his survey required their co-operation. For as long as native people were significant to the agenda of Europeans, they retained some autonomy and their cultures remained intact. When they became irrelevant to the plans of the newcomers, they were shunted aside. They never ceased to assert their claim to the coast, but they were diminished and dispossesed by the forces that Vancouver's survey eventually unleashed.

Though the coast would be changed by his presence, Vancouver himself never knew the magnitude of what he had accomplished. His gravestone in the quiet churchyard in Petersham bears the simple incription: "Captain George Vancouver | Died in the Year 1798 | Aged 40." Half a world away, in Victoria, British Columbia, he stands more portentously atop the dome of the provincial legislative buildings, gazing out upon the coast that he did so much to define. Should we seek any other monument to his work, his chart of the line of coast should be enough. George Vancouver was the first to clearly set down its contours. His exploration put the parameters of place on paper and revealed its reality. He was the one who, perhaps more than anyone else, discovered

> *the problem that is ours and yours*
> *that there is no clear Strait of Anian*
> *to lead us easy back to Europe*
> *that men are isled in ocean or in ice*
> *and are only joined by long endeavour to be joined*[13]

Vancouver showed that, shape it how we will, our history must be worked out on this coastline. While distance has imposed isolation, its raw, wild beauty continues to beckon, and the tide still runs with the ebb and flow of time. Many have followed in the wake of Vancouver, and, crossing the shoreline, some have left their mark on the beaches. And yet the coastline endures. For in the end, there is sea and land.

NOTES

CHAPTER I *Line of Time*

1. W. Kaye Lamb (ed.), *George Vancouver: A Voyage of Discovery to the North Pacific Ocean and Round the World 1791–1795* (London: Hakluyt Society, 1984), pp. 484–85. (Hereafter cited as Vancouver, *Voyage*.)

2. J. C. Beaglehole (ed.), *The Journals of Captain James Cook on His Voyages of Discovery: volume II, The Voyage of the "Resolution" and "Adventure" 1772–1775* (Cambridge: Hakluyt Society, 1969), p. 880.

3. James Cook and James King, *A Voyage to the Pacific Ocean . . . Performed under the Direction of Captains Cook, Clerke, and Gore, in His Majesty's Ships the Resolution and Discovery. In the years 1776, 1777, 1778, 1779, and 1780* (London: G. Nichol and T. Cadell, 1784), 3:438–40.

4. John Kendrick (trans.), *The Voyage of Sutil and Mexicana 1792: The Last Spanish Exploration of the Northwest Coast of America* (Spokane: Arthur H. Clark, 1991), p. 135.

CHAPTER II *First Season: Complications & Convolutions*

1. Lamb, "Introduction" to Vancouver, *Voyage*, p. 62; and Vancouver, *Voyage*, p. 365

2. For an account of Cook's methods see Andrew David (ed.), *The Charts and Coastal Views of Captain Cook's Voyages, volume I, The Voyage of the Endeavour 1768–1771 . . .* (London: Hakluyt Society, 1988), pp. xxix–xxx.

3. J. C. Beaglehole (ed.), *The Journals of Captain James Cook on His Voyages of Discovery: volume III, The Voyage of the "Resolution" and "Discovery" 1776–1780* (Cambridge: Hakluyt Society, 1967), pp. 293–94.

4. Vancouver, *Voyage*, p. 505.

5. Vancouver, *Voyage*, pp. 514–15.

6. Vancouver, *Voyage*, pp. 515–16.

7. Vancouver, *Voyage*, pp. 549–50.

8. Vancouver, *Voyage*, p. 506.

9. Thomas Manby, "A Journal of Vancouver's Voyage," 24 April 1792, p. 70, (photocopy) University of British Columbia Library.

10. Vancouver, *Voyage*, pp. 551–52.

11. Menzies, journal, 6 and 23 June 1792, A. Menzies, "Journal of Vancouver's Voyage, 1790–1794," Ad. ms. 32641, ff.139 and 147, British Library.

12. For this tendency in European attitudes see Robin Fisher, *Contact and Conflict: Indian-European Relations in British Columbia, 1774–1890* (Vancouver: University of British Columbia Press, 1977), pp. 81–82 and 85.

13. Vancouver, *Voyage*, p. 1055.

14. Vancouver, *Voyage*, p. 627.

15. Kendrick, *Voyage of Sutil and Mexicana*, p. 142.

16. Vancouver, *Voyage*, p. 601.

17. Vancouver, *Voyage*, p. 627.

18. Vancouver, *Voyage*, p. 633.

19. Vancouver, *Voyage*, pp. 641–44.

20. Vancouver, *Voyage*, p. 657.

21. Vancouver to Evan Nepean, Under Secretary of State, 7 January 1793, Vancouver, *Voyage*, p. 1580.
22. Vancouver, *Voyage*, p. 682; and Lamb, "Introduction" to Vancouver, *Voyage*, p. 108.
23. John Meares, *Voyages Made in the Years 1788 and 1789, from China to the North West Coast of America...* (London: Logographic Press, 1790), p. 113.
24. Vancouver, *Voyage*, pp. 671, 672, and 683; Menzies, journal, 5 September 1792, ff.190.
25. Vancouver, *Voyage*, p. 671.
26. Manby, "A Journal," July 1792, p. 96.
27. For brief accounts of Hawaiian politics at this time see K. R. Howe, *Where the Waves Fall: A New South Sea Islands History from First Settlement to Colonial Rule* (Sydney and London: Allen & Unwin, 1984), pp. 152–58; and Gavan Daws, *The Shoal of Time: A History of the Hawaiian Islands* (Honolulu: University Press of Hawaii, 1968), pp. 29–44.
28. Vancouver, *Voyage*, p. 856.
29. For an account of the event see Greg Dening, *History's Anthropology: The Death of William Gooch* (Lanham: University Press of America, 1988), pp. xv–xix, 90–95 and *passim*.
30. Vancouver, *Voyage*, p. 898.

CHAPTER III *Second Season: Into the Labyrinth*

1. Vancouver, *Voyage*, p. 1066.
2. Vancouver, *Voyage*, p. 955.
3. Vancouver, *Voyage*, p. 924.
4. Vancouver, *Voyage*, pp. 928, 930, 1006, 957 and 938.
5. Vancouver, *Voyage*, pp. 942–43.
6. Vancouver, *Voyage*, p. 931.
7. Alexander Mackenzie, *The Journals and Letters of Sir Alexander Mackenzie*, ed. W. Kaye Lamb (Cambridge: The Hakluyt Society, 1970), pp. 375–77.
8. On the illness see D. B. Quayle, *Paralytic Shellfish Poisoning in British Columbia*, Fisheries Research Board of Canada Bulletin 168 (Ottawa: Fisheries Research Board, 1969), pp. 4–5 and 14–17; on the earlier instance see Manby, "A Journal," June 1792, p. 89.
9. Vancouver, *Voyage*, pp. 947–48.
10. Lamb, "Introduction" to Vancouver, *Voyage*, pp. 137–38; and Vancouver, *Voyage*, pp. 1011–17.

11. Vancouver, *Voyage*, p. 1017.
12. Vancouver, *Voyage*, p. 1022.
13. Vancouver, *Voyage*, p. 1062.
14. Vancouver, *Voyage*, pp. 1024, 1064, 1062.
15. Vancouver, *Voyage*, pp. 1071–72.
16. Vancouver, *Voyage*, p. 1119.
17. Vancouver, *Voyage*, pp. 1145 and 1147.
18. Vancouver, *Voyage*, p. 1156.
19. Vancouver, *Voyage*, pp. 1176–77.
20. Vancouver, *Voyage*, p. 1160.
21. Vancouver, *Voyage*, p. 1185.
22. Vancouver, *Voyage*, p. 1206.

CHAPTER IV *Third Season: The Shape of Reality*

1. Vancouver, *Voyage*, pp. 1208 and 1217–18.
2. Glyndwr Williams, "Myth and Reality: James Cook and the Theoretical Geography of Northwest America," in Robin Fisher and Hugh Johnston (eds.), *Captain James Cook and His Times* (Vancouver: Douglas & McIntyre, 1979), pp. 60 and 71–74.
3. Beaglehole, *Journals*, III, p. 368.
4. Vancouver, *Voyage*, p. 1243.
5. Lamb, "Introduction," to Vancouver, *Voyage*, p. 169.
6. Vancouver, *Voyage*, p. 1294.
7. See Erna Gunther, *Indian Life on the Northwest Coast of North America as Seen by the Early Explorers and Fur Traders during the Last Decades of the Eighteenth Century* (Chicago and London: University of Chicago Press, 1972), pp. 182–83; and Kaj Birket-Smith, *The Chugach Eskimo*, Nationalmuseets Skrifter Etnografisk Roekke no. 6 (Copenhagen, 1952), pp. 7–8.
8. Vancouver, *Voyage*, pp. 1219, 1224 and 1255.
9. Vancouver, *Voyage*, p. 1235.
10. Vancouver, *Voyage*, pp. 1256, 1241 and 1302.
11. Vancouver, *Voyage*, pp. 1303–4; Beaglehole, *Journals*, III, p. 357n.
12. Vancouver, *Voyage*, p. 1321.
13. Vancouver, *Voyage*, p. 1341.
14. Vancouver, *Voyage*, p. 1321.
15. Vancouver, *Voyage*, pp. 1370 and 1382.
16. Vancouver, *Voyage*, pp. 1370–71.
17. Vancouver, *Voyage*, pp. 1382–83, 1371.
18. Vancouver, *Voyage*, p. 1371.

19. W. K. Lamb (ed.), *Vancouver Discovers Vancouver: An Excerpt from the Rough Logs of Second Lieutenant Peter John Puget* (Burnaby: Vancouver Conference on Exploration and Discovery, [1989]), p. 6.
20. Vancouver, *Voyage*, p. 1030.
21. Vancouver to Stephens, 8 September 1794, Lamb, "Introduction" to Vancouver, *Voyage*, p. 182.
22. Vancouver, *Voyage*, pp. 1399–1406.
23. Vancouver to John Sykes, 3 October 1794, Lamb, "Introduction" to Vancouver, *Voyage*, p. 183.
24. Vancouver, *Voyage*, p. 1411.
25. Vancouver, *Voyage*, pp. 1421–22.

CHAPTER V *The End of Dreaming*

1. Vancouver, *Voyage*, p. 1541.
2. Vancouver, *Voyage*, p. 1539.
3. Michael Lewis, *A Social History of the Navy 1793–1815* (London: Allen and Unwin, 1960), p. 402.
4. Vancouver, *Voyage*, p. 1541.
5. Glyndwr Williams, *The British Search for the Northwest Passage in the Eighteenth Century* (London: Longmans, 1962), pp. 221–25.
6. Bern Anderson, *Surveyor of the Sea: The Life and Voyages of Captain George Vancouver* (Toronto: University of Toronto Press, 1960); Lamb, "Introduction" to Vancouver, *Voyage*, pp. 211–12; John Naish, personal communication with author, 29 May 1991.
7. Vancouver, *Voyage*, p. 1454.
8. Lamb, "Introduction" to Vancouver, *Voyage*, pp. 202, 218–19, 223 and 227–28.
9. Vancouver, *Voyage*, pp. 1303, 1391 and 290 (Vancouver's emphases).
10. O. H. K. Spate, *Paradise Found and Lost: The Pacific Since Magellan, Volume III* (Minneapolis: University of Minnesota Press, 1988), p. 180.
11. Lamb, "Introduction" to Vancouver, *Voyage*, p. 246.
12. Vancouver, *Voyage*, p. 1065.
13. Earle Birney, "Pacific Door," in *Selected Poems 1940–1966* (Toronto/Montreal: McClelland and Stewart, 1966), p. 142. Used by permission of the Canadian Publishers, McClelland & Stewart, Toronto.

SUGGESTIONS FOR FURTHER READING

Anderson, Bern. *Surveyor of the Sea: The Life and Voyages of Captain George Vancouver.* Toronto: University of Toronto Press, 1960.

Beaglehole, J. C., ed. *The Journals of Captain James Cook on His Voyages of Discovery: volume II, The Voyage of the "Resolution" and "Adventure" 1772–1775.* Cambridge: Hakluyt Society, 1969.

Beaglehole, J. C., ed. *The Journals of Captain James Cook on His Voyages of Discovery: volume III, The Voyage of the "Resolution" and "Discovery" 1776–1780.* Cambridge: Hakluyt Society, 1967.

Birket-Smith, Kaj. *The Chugach Eskimo.* Nationalmuseets Skrifter Etnografisk Roekke no. 6. Copenhagen, 1952.

Cook, James, and King, James. *A Voyage to the Pacific Ocean . . . Performed under the Direction of Captains Cook, Clerke, and Gore, in His Majesty's Ships the Resolution and Discovery. In the years 1776, 1777, 1778, 1779, and 1780.* London: G. Nichol and T. Cadell, 1784.

Cook, Warren L. *Flood Tide of Empire: Spain and the Pacific Northwest, 1543–1819.* New Haven and London: Yale University Press, 1973.

Cutter, Donald C. *Malaspina & Galiano: Spanish Voyages to the Northwest Coast, 1791 & 1792.* Vancouver/Toronto: Douglas & McIntyre, 1991.

David, Andrew, ed. *The Charts and Coastal Views of Captain Cook's Voyages, volume I, The Voyage of the Endeavour 1768–1771 . . .* London: Hakluyt Society, 1988.

Daws, Gavan. *The Shoal of Time: A History of the Hawaiian Islands.* Honolulu: University Press of Hawaii, 1968.

Dening, Greg. *History's Anthropology: The Death of William Gooch.* Lanham: University Press of America, 1988.

Fisher, Robin. *Contact and Conflict: Indian-European Relations in British Columbia, 1774–1890.* Vancouver: University of British Columbia Press, 1977.

Fisher, Robin. "Lamb's Vancouver *Voyage,*" *Pacific Northwest Quarterly,* 76 (October 1985): 132–36.

Fisher, Robin, and Johnston, Hugh, eds. *Captain James Cook and His Times.* Vancouver: Douglas & McIntyre, 1979.

Fry, Howard. *Alexander Dalrymple (1737–1808) and the Expansion of British Trade.* London: Frank Cass, 1970.

Gough, Barry M. *Distant Dominion: Britain and the Northwest Coast of North America, 1579–1909.* Vancouver: University of British Columbia Press, 1980.

Gunther, Erna. *Indian Life on the Northwest Coast of North America as Seen by the Early Explorers and Fur Traders during the Last Decades of the Eighteenth Century.* Chicago and London: University of Chicago Press, 1972.

Howe, K. R. *Where the Waves Fall: A New South Sea Islands History from First Settlement to Colonial Rule.* Sydney and London: Allen & Unwin, 1984.

Kendrick, John, trans. *The Voyage of Sutil and Mexicana 1792: The Last Spanish Exploration of the Northwest Coast of America.* Spokane: Arthur H. Clark, 1991.

Lamb, W. Kaye, ed. *George Vancouver: A Voyage of Discovery to the North Pacific Ocean and Round the World 1791–1795.* 4 vols. London: Hakluyt Society, 1984.

Lamb, W. Kaye, ed. *The Journals and Letters of Sir Alexander Mackenzie.* Cambridge: Hakluyt Society, 1970.

Lamb, W. K., ed. *Vancouver Discovers Vancouver: An Excerpt from the*

Rough Logs of Second Lieutenant Peter John Puget. Burnaby: Vancouver Conference on Exploration and Discovery, [1989].

Lewis, Michael. *A Social History of the Navy 1793–1815.* London: Allen and Unwin, 1960.

Mackay, David. *In the Wake of Cook: Exploration, Science & Empire, 1780–1801* London: Croom Helm, 1985.

Meares, John. *Voyages Made in the Years 1788 and 1789, from China to the North West Coast of America. . .* London: Logographic Press, 1790.

Moziño, José Mariano, *Noticias de Nutka: An Account of Nootka Sound in 1792.* Seattle and London: University of Washington Press, 1991.

Newcombe, C. F. *Menzies' Journal of Vancouver's Voyage: April to October, 1792.* Archives of British Columbia Memoir no. V. Victoria: King's Printer, 1923.

Quayle, D. B. *Paralytic Shellfish Poisoning in British Columbia,* Fisheries Research Board of Canada Bulletin 168. Ottawa: Fisheries Research Board, 1969.

Richards, Paul. *King's Lynn.* Chichester: Phillimore, 1990.

Ritchie, G. S. *The Admiralty Chart British Naval Hydrography in the Nineteenth Century.* London: Hollis & Carter, 1967.

Spate, O. H. K. *Paradise Found and Lost: The Pacific Since Magellan, Volume III.* Minneapolis: University of Minnesota Press, 1988.

Suttles, Wayne. *Handbook of North American Indians, Volume 7 Northwest Coast.* Washington: Smithsonian Institution, 1990.

Tippett, Maria, and Cole, Douglas. *From Desolation to Splendour: Changing Perceptions of the British Columbia Landscape.* Toronto/Vancouver: Clarke, Irwin & Company, 1977.

Williams, Glyndwr. *The British Search for the Northwest Passage in the Eighteenth Century.* London: Longmans, 1962.

Williams, Glyndwr. *The Expansion of Europe in the Eighteenth Century: Overseas Rivalry, Discovery and Exploration.* New York: Walker and Company, 1966.

LIST OF COLOUR PLATES

INDEX